A Guide to

Everyday Economic Statistics

Eighth Edition

Gary E. Clayton

Martin Gerhard Giesbrecht

Feng Guo

Mc
Graw
Hill
Education

A GUIDE TO EVERYDAY ECONOMIC STATISTICS, EIGHTH EDITION

Published by McGraw-Hill Education, 2 Penn Plaza, New York, NY 10121. Copyright © 2019 by McGraw-Hill Education. All rights reserved. Printed in the United States of America. Previous editions © 2010, 2004, and 2001. No part of this publication may be reproduced or distributed in any form or by any means, or stored in a database or retrieval system, without the prior written consent of McGraw-Hill Education, including, but not limited to, in any network or other electronic storage or transmission, or broadcast for distance learning.

Some ancillaries, including electronic and print components, may not be available to customers outside the United States.

This book is printed on acid-free paper.

1 2 3 4 5 6 QVS 22 21 20 19 18

ISBN   978-1-260-02541-5
MHID   1-260-02541-1

Portfolio Manager: *Katie Hoenicke*
Product Developer: *Kevin White*
Content Project Manager: *Melissa M. Leick*
Buyer: *Susan K. Culbertson*
Content Licensing Specialist: *Lorraine Buczek*
Cover Image: *Shutterstock / isak55*
Compositor: *Aptara®, Inc.*

mheducation.com/highered

By the way, you won't have to read this book consecutively from beginning to end, although that is OK too. But keep it handy! Do so even in good times when it may seem less urgent to keep an eye on economic statistics. Remember, we may put off watching our diets or keeping tabs on our blood pressures when we are in robust health. But, as more than a few of us have learned, this is also a time when concern about our personal well-being is critical. Doing likewise with our economic statistics not only helps keep track of our economic health, it may also enable us to move from understanding to the final level of sophistication: call it wisdom.

That's what this little book is all about. Use it well, and use it often.

Gary E. Clayton

Martin Gerhard Giesbrecht

Feng Guo

About the Authors

Gary E. Clayton is Professor and former Chair of the Economics & Finance Department at Northern Kentucky University. His Ph.D. in economics is from the University of Utah and he is the only American with an Honorary Doctorate from the People's Friendship University of Russia (PFUR) in Moscow. He has appeared on numerous radio and television programs and for two years was a regular guest commentator on economic statistics for NPR's *Marketplace*. In addition to his other writings and newspaper commentary, he has published five textbooks in the middle school, high school and college markets, including the best-selling *Understanding Economics* with McGraw-Hill Education. Professor Clayton's web portal, www.EconSources.com, was described as "among the most useful [sites] on the web" by the Federal Reserve Bank of Boston's *Ledger*.

Dr. Clayton has taught international business and economics to students in London, Austria, and Australia. He is interested in the economic advancement of developing nations and in 2006 helped organize a micro loan project in Uganda. He is a year 2000 Freedoms Foundation Leavey Award winner for Excellence in Private Enterprise Education, an Association of Real Estate License Law Officials (ARELLO) national Consumer Education Award winner, and the recipient of a national teaching award from the National Council on Economic Education. In 2005 Dr. Clayton was the recipient of Northern Kentucky University's Frank Sinton Milburn Outstanding Professor Award.

Martin Gerhard Giesbrecht is Professor Emeritus of Economics at Northern Kentucky University. He has taught and/or conducted research at Stanford University, the University of Chicago, Harvard University, Indiana University, National Chengchi University (Taiwan), Rutgers University, and Wilmington College. His doctoral degree (cum laude) was earned at the University of Munich, Germany, which he attended on a Fulbright Grant. Making economics accessible, intellectually enlightening, and even entertaining is the mission of Martin Giesbrecht's professional life. All of his 12 books, including this one, and his many shorter articles, some of which have also appeared in German and Chinese, are dedicated to that end, as are his weekly radio commentaries on WNKU and WMKV.

Because he writes and speaks in a way that people can understand, the Society of Professional Journalism bestowed the Award for Excellence on him in 1993. He has also won awards from the German-American Chamber of Commerce, the National Aeronautics and Space Administration (NASA), the American Society for Engineering Education, the National Science Foundation, the General Electric Foundation, the Ford Foundation, the U.S. Small Business

Administration, and the National Endowment for the Humanities, among others. He is especially gratified that the ΦΒΛ (Future Business Leaders) Fraternity voted him their favorite professor on the NKU campus.

 Feng Guo is Chief Economist at Heaven-Sent Capital Management Group, one of largest private equity firms in China, and Managing Partner & Head of the Research Institute at Zhejiang Silicon Paradise Asset Management Group. Previously, Dr. Guo was Chief Representative of Asia Pacific and Chief China Economist at the Institute of International Finance (IIF) in Washington DC for six years. He also worked as a Senior Research Economist at the Center for Economic Analysis and Development at Northern Kentucky University. From 2004 to 2008, Dr. Guo was a Research Economist with The Conference Board in New York City where he specialized in the development of business cycle indices for China and in forecasting aggregate economic activities for East Asian economies.

Dr. Guo has published numerous research reports and peer-reviewed academic papers on East Asia's macroeconomics, financial markets, and economic developments. Dr. Guo obtained his Ph.D. in Economics from the Graduate Center, City University of New York, and his master's degree in Economics from Rissho University in Tokyo, Japan.

Acknowledgments

For almost two decades now, through the many editions of this little book, we have benefited from the generous help, advice, comments, and suggestions of hundreds of economists, statisticians, journalists, financiers, students, leaders in industry and government, and other interested readers. We continue to be enormously grateful to them all, as we are to McGraw-Hill for working with us from the beginning to bring you this little Guide. And finally, we are especially indebted to our families for putting up with us during the weeks and months when they were pushed aside while we worked on manuscript and deadlines—we could not have done it without them! And, of course, any errors that remain are entirely our responsibility.

Table of Contents

Chapter 1

INTRODUCTION

How the Statistics in This Book Were Chosen

We need economic statistics to know how we are doing, and we need to know how we are doing in order to figure out how to get where we want to go. Decision making requires knowledge, and knowledge is the only logical basis of action. That is why we need economic statistics.

The problem is that there are literally millions of statistical series! At the personal level, each of us could probably generate a dozen series from our grocery receipts, odometer readings, telephone bills, and electricity bills. Every business, town, city, county, and industry could do, and often does, the same in its own field of operation.

Even the broad-based measures of economic statistics, those that deal with whole states, regions, and nations, number into the thousands. In fact, there are now so many national statistics that the U.S. Census Bureau can no longer publish all of them in its comprehensive annual *Statistical Abstract of the United States.*[1]

Yet, only a handful of economic statistical series are dealt with in this book. Why?

First and most obvious, there is such a thing as too much information. It can prevent us from seeing the forest for all the trees.

---

[1] Even though the *Abstract* has not been published since 2012, complete copies of the *Statistical Abstract* from 1879 to 2012 are available on the Census Bureau's Statistical Abstracts Series website at https://www.census.gov/library/publications/time-series/statistical_abstracts.html. For more current data, the site advises readers to "refer to the organizations cited in the source notes for each table of the [appropriate] *Abstract.*"

Second, many statistical series, like one detailing our own personal electricity consumption, are just not interesting to everyone.

Third, many statistical series are compiled and published too late to be of much more than historical interest.

Finally, many statistical series are not reported regularly in the press and broadcast media, and are therefore of less interest.

However, other statistics have extremely high profiles. Some, like the Dow Jones Industrial Average, are reported daily on television, radio, in newspapers, and on the Internet. Others, like the prime rate, are mentioned less frequently, but still receive prominent attention. Even others, like auto sales, are important because they tell us how a particular sector of the economy is performing.

If we want to know how we are doing or where we are headed, even a handful of series are usually more than enough. They include most of the major economic indicators that are important all of the time. Consumer confidence, the consumer price index, and the unemployment rate would certainly be in the top half-dozen of anyone's list of key economic statistics. Many others are important most of the time, and the rest are important at least some of the time.

We may not have selected everyone's favorite statistics for this little book—and for that we apologize—but we are driven by a positive philosophy of wanting to describe "what is" rather than a normative one of "what should be." The popular press may neglect some statistics when they should not be, while others are widely reported when there is less reason to do so. However, the objective here is to provide a guide to those series that *do* receive the attention rather than to the ones that *should*.

A Frame of Reference

The main measure of overall economic and business activity is gross domestic product (GDP), whose fluctuations are the most important gauge of good times or bad times that we have. Because GDP is defined as the total dollar value of all new final goods and services produced in a country during a one-year period, GDP is to be understood as a final, bottom-line accounting measure, an economic result, rather than as an indicator of things to come.

Many of the statistics reviewed in this book measure either the whole or parts of GDP. Other statistics, The Conference Board's Leading Economic Index preeminent among them, serve better as signals of things to come. There are also more specialized series, such as the Standard & Poor's 500 (S&P 500), that serve both as general indicators of future economic activity and as first-order indicators for their own industries. Finally, we have other series such as new housing starts that provide important information for their own industries, but less value as indicators of future economic activity.

As we peruse the formal world of economic statistics, bear in mind that they cannot be evaluated in a vacuum. Statistical series need a background, or a frame of reference, so that they can be put in proper perspective. This the book attempts to do. Sometimes the frame of reference is discussed in terms of the historical development and evolution of the series. Or, the perspective may take the form of a detailed discussion of the way the statistic is measured and compiled. The frame of reference may also be the way the particular indicator or statistic relates to other developments in the economy. In the end, our goal is to provide a perspective that allows for proper interpretation and application of the particular series.

Of particular interest are the three types of indicators—leading, coincident, and lagging—shown in Figure 1-1. The name given to each refers to the way the series moves in relation to changes in overall economic activity. For example, the series marked "leading indicator" turns down (gets worse) before the economy enters a recession (indicated by the shaded area in the figure) and turns up (gets better) before the expansion begins.

The "lagging indicator" series behaves just the opposite—it turns down after the economy enters a recession, and up after the recovery is underway. A coincident indicator neither leads nor lags. Instead, its timing is such that it turns down when the economy turns down, and up when the economy turns up.

Sometimes a series may lead a peak (a relative high) and/or a trough (a relative low) in the economy, and at other times it may lag a peak and/or trough. When this happens, the series is simply less useful for forecasting purposes.

Whenever possible, the economic series examined in this book are plotted against the historical background of recessions and

Figure 1-1
Coincident, Leading, and Lagging Indicators

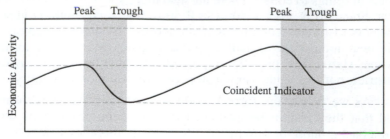

Coincident Indicator

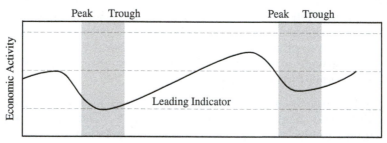

Leading Indicator

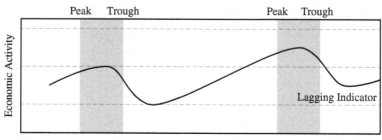

Lagging Indicator

Economists use the convention of shading recessionary periods to distinguish them from periods of expansion. Economic series are classified as leading, coincident, or lagging indicators depending on how their turning points—their peaks and troughs—compare to changes in the overall economy.

Leading indicators get most of the attention because they tend to change direction before the economy goes up or down, and in so doing give us a warning as to where the economy may be headed.

expansions in the manner illustrated in Figure 1-1. As will be seen, many series behave like those in the figure, although the timing of the turning points will vary considerably. Others will appear to have little, if any, relationship to changes in the overall economy. Even so, we feel that the presentation is useful if you are to make your own judgments about the importance of the series.

Finally, we also provide a brief summary of the statistical series that includes its status as an economic indicator, the source agency that compiles the data, the frequency of release, and other key information at the end of every section. In addition, current updates to most of these series, along with press releases, data retrieval tools, background articles, and even related web sites can be found on the *www.EconSources.com* website.

The Many Faces of Economic Statistics

The task of interpreting economic statistics might seem to be a simple one: just take the numbers and describe how they changed from one period to the next. Unfortunately, it's not always that easy because most statistical series can be reported in a number of ways.

To illustrate, consider a hypothetical report stating that total sales increased by 5 percent from $800 billion to $840 billion over a recent 12-month period. If the report is in terms of current prices, and many initial reports are released this way, then it stands to reason that some of the $40 billion increase is due to inflation.

To compensate for inflation, sales can be measured in terms of "real," "constant," or "chain-linked" dollars using prices that prevailed in an earlier base year.[2] If 2009 is used as the base year, the same report could be worded like this: "In terms of chained (2009) prices, total sales increased from $720 billion to $738 billion for the most recent year." This time the increase of $18 billion is only a 2.5 percent gain, so half of the current dollar increase was due to inflation, the other half was due to real growth.

---

[2] In 1996, the U.S. Department of Commerce switched from a system of base-year fixed prices to a system using chain-weighted geometric averages with 1992 as the reference year. In 1999, the base year was rebased to 1996 and is now 2009 although it will again be updated before long. This technique is described more fully in the Appendix.

   Most series that are susceptible to the distortions of inflation are reported in both current (nominal) and real (constant 2009 or chained 2009) dollar amounts. Both kinds of information are valuable—if used correctly—although the availability of both means that statistics such as sales can be reported in a number of different and seemingly confusing ways[3]:

- the final *current* or *nominal* dollar value of total sales ($840 billion)
- the change in the *current* or *nominal* dollar value of total sales ($40 billion)
- the final *chained, constant,* or *real* dollar value of total sales ($738 billion in 2009 dollars)
- the change in *chained, constant,* or *real* dollar value of total sales ($18 billion in 2009 dollars)
- the percentage change in the *current* or *nominal* dollar sales (5.0 percent, or $40 billion/$800 billion)
- the percentage change in *chain-weighted, constant,* or *real dollar sales* (2.5 percent, or $18 billion/$720 billion in 2009 dollars)

   We have a similar problem when numbers are converted to an index, such as the consumer price index, the producer price index, or any other index. For example, suppose that the index under consideration has a base year of 1977 = 100 and currently stands at 145. If the index goes to 146 in the next month, there is an increase of 1 over the base period activity, or a 0.69 percent increase in the index over the previous month (1/145 = 0.0069). If the index were to grow at the same rate for each of the next 11 months, the annualized rate would be 8.6 percent.[4]

---

[3] Unfortunately the terms that economists use to describe numbers that are—or are not—distorted by inflation can be an endless source of confusion. While we tend to use some terms interchangeably in the text, the following guide may be of help when it comes to sorting out the differences. Specifically:

- Series adjusted for inflation are described as being in *constant dollar, real dollar,* or *chained dollar* amounts (where chaining is the inflation adjustment technique used).
- Series *not* adjusted for inflation are described as being in *current* or *nominal* dollar amounts. If nothing is said about the series, as in "GDP this year is expected to be $20 trillion," then *current* (unadjusted) numbers are assumed.

[4] The series is compounded monthly, so the correct computation is as follows:

$$\text{Annualized growth} = (1 + \text{monthly percentage change})^{12} - 1$$
$$= (1 + 0.0069)^{12} - 1 = 0.086$$

Because of compounding, you cannot multiply the monthly percentage change of 0.0069 by 12 to get an annualized rate, although this mistake is often made!

Using the numbers in the preceding paragraph, we can see that the change in any index can be reported in several different ways:

- the *absolute level* of the index (145)
- the *absolute change* in the level of the index from period to period (1)
- the *relative percentage change* from the previous period (0.69 percent)
- an *annualized projection* of the current period percentage change (8.6 percent)

In general, the relative percentage change is the most useful, with the annualized version coming in next. However, the reader should be advised that even these lists are not exclusive. For example, sometimes the change in the level of the index is compared to a period 12 months earlier. If the new level of 146 is 10 points higher than it was 12 months ago, then we could also say that the annual increase was closer to 7.35 percent.

Abusing Economic Statistics

The governments of most modern, industrialized nations of the free world—the United States among the best of them—enjoy a remarkable reputation for producing honest statistics. Many of these same countries also have a number of nongovernmental agencies that produce high-quality statistical series as part of a public service effort to gain acclaim and acceptance for their organizations. In some nations however, statistics are exaggerated, underreported, or simply faked for political or ideological reasons. When this happens, the usefulness of the statistics is radically reduced. Whether they know it or not, it is also a tragic loss to those nations that support this type of activity.

In the United States, our statistics tend to be brutally honest. Agencies that report their statistics normally publish release schedules months in advance of the actual release, and the methodology used to compile the series is remarkably open. As a result, there is not even the slightest hint that the release of new statistical figures is delayed in order to prevent some political or commercial embarrassment.

Abuse, however, does occur.

Perhaps the most common abuse of economic statistics is to apply them to situations for which they were never intended. For example, some series with little, if any, relationship to movements of the overall economy are often treated as if they are significant predictors of future changes in GDP. Personal income in current dollars, discussed in detail in Chapter 2, is one such example. The historical record shows that personal income almost always goes up, even when the economy is in recession.[5] Even so, increases in personal income are dutifully reported and widely heralded by the press each time they are released.

Other series are treated as indicators of future economic activity when, in fact, they are actually coincident or lagging indicators. Interest rates can be cited in this context, especially the prime rate which consistently lags changes in real GDP. Changing interest rates certainly affect selected sectors of the economy, especially housing, automobiles, and to some extent stock prices, but changing interest rates are of little use in predicting future changes in the direction of the overall economy.

Yet another abuse is to focus on nominal dollar values when the real, or inflation-adjusted, figures give a better picture of the underlying changes. Unfortunately, various government agencies sometimes contribute to this problem because the nominal dollar data and the price deflators needed to adjust the data are not available at the same time. When the U.S. Department of Commerce releases its mid-month *Advance Monthly Retail Sales* report, the data are adjusted for seasonal, holiday, and trading day differences, but not for inflation. By the time inflation-adjusted figures are finally available, the initial change in retail sales has already been reported and the new figures are of little interest to the media.

Finally, we should note that the media often report on new economic figures without giving us enough information to evaluate the significance of the numbers. It is not at all unusual to hear that a particular index has gone up, say, 4 points, without any mention of the overall level of the index. Four points on a basis of 40 is one thing, but 4 points on an index with a value of 400 may be quite another. In fact, changes in the Dow Jones Industrial Average are often reported this way, as in "the market was up today, increasing a total of 60 points."

---

[5] The Great Recession of 2008–09 was an exception in that personal income suffered four quarterly declines. See the discussion of disposable personal income in both current and constant dollars on pages 33–35.

Using Economic Statistics

Some decision making may require an understanding of other economic conditions, perhaps those that occur at a regional or industry level. Even if the data you need are not described in these chapters (as most of the statistics in this book pertain to the national economy), you should be able to use the methods described here to build your own set of economic indicators.

If you do, remember that every statistical series has its own distinct personality. If you want to use a series, examine it carefully and try to see how it relates to your own situation. For example, are series measured in real, rather than nominal, dollars better for your application? Also, you might examine the series to see if changes in the series are more important than the absolute level of the series.

And, what about the timing of the series? If it lags, then it may not be of much help. If it leads, then you may have to spend more time trying to anticipate its movements. If you need regional or industry-specific data, don't forget to look for other sources of data generated by state departments of economic development, chambers of commerce, economic development districts, local universities, and industry and trade publications.

One practical way of organizing economic statistics for your own use is to build your own historical database of the statistical series that are especially important to you. You can do this with an appropriate spreadsheet program on your personal computer and then chart or otherwise present the results. Yearly entries may or may not be sufficient for the bygone years, but quarterly and monthly data for more recent times will keep you more up-to-date.

To monitor overall economic conditions, you may want to keep tabs on GDP, the consumer price index, the unemployment rate, or several other series, such as the Leading Economic Index (LEI). To zero in on your own individual area of concern, focus on those series that affect this area more directly. For example, you would examine consumer spending and retail sales if your concern is retail marketing, or the Dow Jones Industrial Average and Standard & Poor's 500 if you are more concerned with the stock market.

As your sophistication grows, this accumulation of statistical data will not only reveal the current state of affairs to you, but you will also begin to be able to discern the development of trends. Being able to do this on your own, rather than relying on the news media, gives you that decisive competitive edge that is so important in today's business world. It's mighty useful in your personal affairs too.

Don't be afraid to be creative. If the statistics enable you to perceive your economic reality, your economic reality may also enable you to anticipate the statistics. This can be very useful. For example, if your decision is to refinance a mortgage, and if you are waiting for the lowest possible rates, it helps to know that interest rates usually go down during a recession and continue to go down well into the subsequent recovery.

So, if the economy appears to be just entering a recession, it might be wise to postpone the refinancing for another year or so. Or, if the expansion is well underway, you may want to refinance immediately since interest rates have a history of increasing late in the recovery. In either case, knowledge of how a series relates to the overall economy can be helpful in a number of ways.

Finally, bear in mind that—until you become more familiar with the statistics in this book—you don't even have to be an expert to know if the economy is in a recession or an expansion. Just stay tuned to the news, and the media will keep you abreast of developments. Of course the media may miss the beginning or ending of a recession by six months or so—but be especially suspect of politicians who make proclamations about the state of the economy as they may be trying to distort the real situation for personal political gain. For the most part, however, those who report on national economic developments in the media usually do a reasonably good job of keeping us posted on the state of the economy.

And Beware of Forecasts!

With all of this said, we should also point out that none of this is a formal theory nor a method for making forecasts. Much longer books than this have dealt unsuccessfully with that subject. But we do encounter many large and small forecasts in our daily lives, and these often contain fertile opportunities for making statistical trouble. Be forewarned! Here are some things to look out for:

Point Forecasts These are the most common, but they are often wrong because outcomes are unlikely to reach the precisely predicted point. For example, if we predict that the GDP next year will be $20 trillion, we have an almost 100 percent chance of being wrong because next year's GDP might turn up to be $20 trillion and 1 cent or any other such number. It is better to make an *interval forecast* that next year's GDP will be $20 trillion, give or take $50 billion.

Probability Forecasts It is even better to say that next year's GDP has an 85 percent probability of being between $19.95 trillion and $21.05 trillion. The higher the probability, the more believable the forecast will appear to be, assuming that the forecaster is reputable.

Conditional Forecasts "There is an 85 percent probability that next year's GDP will be between $19.95 trillion and $21.05 trillion if the Federal Reserve System does not raise the primary credit rate" is a conditional forecast because all bets are off if the Fed does raise the primary credit rate. This not only gives the forecaster an "out" if the forecast turns out to be wrong, but it also makes the forecast a bit less useful to the user.

Time Series Forecasts A series of forecasts that march into the future by convenient time steps—months, quarters, or years—are much more complicated than a single-event forecast. For example, forecasting that "GDP next year will grow at an annual rate of 4 percent during the first 6 months and then slow to 3 percent in the last half of the year" is actually making two forecasts. Since the second one is probably dependent on the accurate of the first, this kind of forecasting can be tricky.

Extrapolation Forecasts Extrapolating a constant rate of growth from a series of monthly or quarterly changes often appears as a kind of time series forecast. However, this type of forecast is even more problematic than a time series forecast as "Anyone who believes that exponential growth can go on forever in a finite world is either a madman or an economist."[6]

Weighted Moving Average Forecasts If a particular series is subject to considerable fluctuation, a moving average with specific weights assigned to earlier periods can be used to smooth the data. When this technique is adapted to forecasting, it is easier to predict the next number in the average since a portion of the data used to construct it is already in hand. And, with our attention focused on the moving average, the forecaster can even be excused if the next new observation "deviates" from the mean.

Many of the forecasts that we encounter in the daily news have considerable value. Many others, however, have little or no value since we are not clear as to what kind of forecast they are or how they have been constructed. They may use hedging or waffling language that, when carefully examined, pulls the rug of credibility out from underneath them. Even worse, they could be based on other statistics that may not be well suited for the forecast being made.

---

[6] Economist Kenneth Boulding, quoted in "Out in the Sort" by John McPhee, *The New Yorker*, 18 April 2005, page 167.

A Final Word

Throughout, this book tries to be ideologically and theoretically neutral, or at least conventional. Notice that the economic indicators described in the following chapters are grouped primarily by economic function rather than by alphabet or other method. This is to recognize implicitly that, while no formal theoretical or ideological statement is intended, our economy is nevertheless a functioning system made up of identifiable parts that somehow work together.

And remember: we should never become so blinded by the apparent numerical precision and by the "scientific," "theoretical," or "official" nature of these economic indicators that we ignore our own sensitivity to economic and business conditions. Our own observations may be rather parochial, but they are immediate and undisputably real. Keeping an eye on the amount of construction activity in the neighborhood where we live, the type of cars that we and our neighbors drive, the intensity of traffic on our streets, how hard or easy it is to find a place to park, what and how much people are buying in the stores where we shop, the number of layoffs or job promotions among our friends and acquaintances, the level of maintenance and upkeep in our surrounding buildings and grounds, and even the changes in the frequency of marriages and new babies in our communities can all be very revealing. We ourselves are, after all, living daily in the very economy we are trying to understand.

This economic awareness, this "feel" for business conditions, should be extended to our interpretations of statistical series as well. We can examine the way statistical series are constructed, and we can look at the historical record to see how they behave. But in the end, it comes down to developing a feel for what they really tell us. This is why forecasting is, and will likely remain, an art rather than a science.

Chapter 2

TOTAL OUTPUT and INCOME

Gross Domestic Product

The most comprehensive measure of production is **gross domestic product (GDP)**—the market value of all final goods, services, and structures produced in one year by labor and property located in the United States, regardless of who owns the resources.[1] GDP is the summary statistic that comes from our national income and product accounts (NIPA) compiled by the Bureau of Economic Analysis (BEA) in the U.S. Department of Commerce. The NIPA and its components are the results of the most exhaustive statistical collection efforts ever undertaken—and collectively they give us our most comprehensive view of the economy's performance.

The need to know more about the economy became apparent during the Great Depression of the 1930s when it was discovered that our information about overall economic performance was limited at best. Pioneering work on GDP was done by Dr. Simon Kuznets of the National Bureau of Economic Research in the 1930s and 1940s. Later, he received the Nobel Prize for his efforts. The measure has been refined and improved since then, and in December of 1999, the U.S. Department of Commerce announced that the development of GDP and NIPA was "its achievement of the century."[2]

---

[1] In 1991, GDP replaced *gross national product (GNP)*, a measure of the total income produced in one year with labor and property supplied by U.S. residents, regardless of where the resources are located. The conversion to GDP made the measurement of total output consistent with the system of accounts used by the World Bank and most other industrial nations.

[2] "GDP: One of the Great Inventions of the 20th Century," *Survey of Current Business*, January 2000.

Estimating GDP

The concept of GDP is fairly easy to grasp. Basically, if we could determine how many goods, services, and structures are produced in a year, and if we multiplied them by their prices, we could add them up to get a dollar measure of GDP. This is how the advance first quarter 2017 estimate of $19,027.6 billion, or $19.0 trillion, in Table 2-1 below was derived.

Table 2-1
Computation of GDP in Current Dollars

GDP in Current Prices (billions of dollars):

Annual Domestic Output		Quantity in Millions	Current Prices	Value in Billions of $
Goods:	Automobiles	10	$39,000	$390.0
	Chairs	8	50	0.4
	..... Other	—	—	—
Services:	Legal	12	800	9.6
	Child care/wk	4	100	0.4
	..... Other	—	—	—
Structures:	Residential	4	240,000	960.0
	Commercial	2	340,000	680.0
	..... Other	—	—	—
	GDP in current dollars			*$19,027.6*

However, the size and complexity of any economy makes this simple computation a monumental task. It is so difficult, in fact, that it is more accurate to say that GDP is "estimated" rather than measured. So, exactly what data do economists use when it comes to estimating the size of our GDP?

Fortunately, data from a wide variety of sources are available to estimate GDP and the NIPA components. The primary source is the Economic Census which covers virtually the entire economy. This census is updated every 5 years with most recent one being conducted in 2012.[3] Various other sources are also used to supplement the underlying five-year estimates. For example, income is derived from

---

[3] Prior to 2012, the various censuses that covered manufacturing, retail and wholesale trade, agriculture, construction, transportation, and government, were all available in printed form. Since 2012 they have been conveniently available on the Census Bureau's website.

the Quarterly Census of Employment and Wages that is conducted by the Bureau of Labor Statistics (BLS). This report covers more than 98 percent of U.S. jobs and provides income data from wages, salaries, stock options and even executive bonuses.

In addition, the Internal Revenue Service provides estimates for corporate profits; the Census Bureau conducts retail trade surveys to update shifts in consumer spending patterns; and, the Customs Bureau provides data on exports and imports. In addition to the major 5-year revisions, new data are added as they become available and are incorporated in their annual updates.

Other entries, as in the case of owner-occupied housing, are imputed. For example, someone who rents an apartment makes a periodic payment to cover the value of housing services received, whereas the owner of a home does not. To accurately reflect the value of all housing services in GDP, the BEA imputes the rental value of owner-occupied housing.

We could go on, but the bottom line is that the estimation of GDP is a complex undertaking; so, we'll leave the measurement problem to the statisticians and focus on other matters instead.

Quarterly Revisions

GDP is reported quarterly, but then it is updated twice in the next two months, so what accounts for this?

Basically, the BEA faces a trade-off between quality and timing. Because the data used to compute GDP are only available after a lag, the longer the lag in reporting GDP, the better the estimate because more complete data are available. However, some users are more interested in getting the quarterly estimates as soon as possible, so the BEA releases three estimates for every quarter[4]:

Advance—released near the end of the *first* month after the end of the quarter and is based on source data that are incomplete or subject to further revision.

Second—released near end of the *second* month after end of the quarter and is based on more detailed source material as they become available.

Third—released near the end of the *third* month after the end of the quarter and is based on the most complete source data.

---

[4] The three releases were previously known as Advance, Preliminary, and Final.

Figure 2-1 shows the three GDP estimates from the second quarter of 2015 into the first quarter of 2017. Each quarterly estimate is reported on an annualized basis—which means that this is the rate at which the economy would grow for a 12-month period if the growth in the other three quarters were the same as the current one. Since this is seldom the case, the final figures for the year will be slightly different.[5]

Despite the frequent revisions, they provide surprisingly reliable results. One BEA study found that each of the estimates— Advance, Second, and Third—provide reliable indications of the *direction* of real GDP change 97 percent of the time. In addition, they provide reliable indications of the *rate* of change (accelerating or decelerating rates of growth) about 75 percent of the time.[6] When all

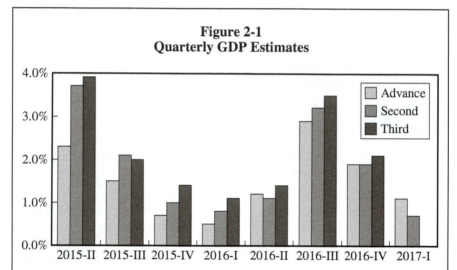

Figure 2-1
Quarterly GDP Estimates

Monthly GDP revisions may vary modestly from one month to the next. Historically, the average revision—without regard to sign—from the advance to the third estimate was plus or minus 1.1 percent. On this basis, the final estimate for 2017-I should fall between 1.8 and −0.4 percent of the advance estimate.

---

[5] The final figures for the year may also include statistical and methodological improvements not reflected in the quarterly estimates.

[6] See Dennis J. Fixler, and Bruce T. Grimm, "Reliability of GDP and Related NIPA Estimates," *Survey of Current Business*, January 2002. The survey covered a 68-quarter period beginning in 1983 and ending in 2000.

of these factors are taken into account, it turns out that the advance estimate for any given quarter—despite the fact that it is revised almost continually—is a fairly reliable statistic.

These revisions mean that we never have the luxury of just adding the latest GDP numbers to an existing time series such as that shown in Figure 2-2 on page 24. Instead, we always have to obtain the most recent estimates for the whole series regardless of whether our interest is in long-term GDP trends or simply in monthly changes from one quarter to the next.[7]

Current vs. Constant Dollar or Real GDP

So far we have covered some of the issues related to getting a reasonable estimate of GDP at a given point in time. However, now we need to consider the way in which inflation can distort comparisons of GDP in different periods—which means that we have to make a distinction between current and constant dollar, or real, GDP.

If GDP is valued using the prices of the period in which the transactions occurred, then the measure is simply *GDP*, *GDP in current prices,* or *nominal GDP*—which unfortunately gives us three ways of saying the same thing.[8]

However, there are times when we want to compare the GDP in one period with the GDP in another. This is easily done, but first we have to recognize that prices have probably changed between the two periods, and that these changes will have biased the resulting

---

[7] A 1999 benchmark revision was made to treat software purchases as a capital investment, rather than to treat it as a business expense. This revision caused an increase in the level of GDP that extended back to 1959.

[8] We don't want to belabor the point, but we know that these terms can be a constant source of confusion for our students, so we'd like suggest the following guide to separating *current* and *real* dollar amounts:

> Dollar values *not* adjusted for inflation are described as being in *current* or *nominal* dollar amounts. For example, if nothing is said about a report, as in "GDP this year is expected to be $22 trillion," then this year's dollar values are assumed. And, if GDP was estimated at $20 trillion two years ago, then GDP was estimated using the prices that prevailed in that year.

> Dollar values adjusted for inflation are described as being in *constant dollar*, *real dollar*, or *chained dollar* amounts where chaining is the adjustment technique used to remove the distortions caused by inflation. See "Chain Weighting" in the Appendix, pages 169–172, for more on this topic.

comparison. As a result, economists have introduced the concept of "real" GDP to remove these price distortions.

Real GDP is estimated for different periods by using the same set of prices to value the output in each. By using the same set of prices, any difference between GDP totals *must* be due to actual changes in the quantity of goods, services, and structures produced—hence the term *real* GDP. Clearly, the difference cannot be due to inflation because the same set of prices was used for both periods.[9]

The BEA currently uses year 2009 base year prices, but it really doesn't matter which year is used as a base year as long as the same set of prices are used when making comparisons. So when a set of constant year 2009 base-year prices are used, the measure is called *real GDP*, or *GDP in constant (2009) dollars*—even though there is nothing otherwise "real" about the computation.

Table 2-2 illustrates both types of computations for the U.S. economy in the first quarter of 2017 (usually denoted 2017-I). Suppose that the items in the quantity column represent actual amounts produced in that year. If output is valued at prices that existed at that time, the total value of production—or GDP in current dollars—is taking place at an annual rate of $19,027.6 billion. In the bottom part of the table, the same output is computed using smaller 2009 chain weighted prices to give us a value of $16,861.6 billion.[10]

Table 2-2 clearly shows that constant or real dollar GDP in part (B) is smaller than in (A) only because prices in 2009 are smaller than the prices in 2017. The difference in GDP for the two measures was *not* due to a change in quantities column.

The advantage of using constant dollar prices is that it enables us to compare the annual rate of total output in the first quarter of 2017 to the third quarter of 2005, or to any other year and quarter

---

[9] A favorite question economists like to use in the classroom goes something like this: "If an economy produces 1000 widgets in one year at a price of $10 each, and if it produces 1000 widgets in the next year at a price of $20 each, did real GDP increase?

The answer is *no* because the real output of the economy, 1000 widgets in both years, did not change. However, nominal GDP doubled because $10,000 of widgets were produced in the first year while $20,000 of widgets were produced in the second year. This example clearly shows that the increase in GDP, i.e. *current* or *nominal* GDP, was due to the inflationary increase of prices from $10 to $20.

[10] The phrase "chain-weighted" or "chain-linked" refers to the manner in which percentage increases are computed from one year to the next. Chain weighting uses prices from both years to compute a geometric mean called the "Fisher Ideal." A brief example of this computation also appears in the Appendix on pages 169–172.

Table 2-2
Computation of GDP in Current *and* Constant (Chained) Dollars, 2017-I

(A) GDP in Current Prices (billions of dollars):

Annual Domestic Output		Quantity in Millions	Current Prices	Value in Billions of $
Goods:	Automobiles	10	$39,000	$390.0
	Chairs	8	50	0.4
	..... Other	—	—	—
Services:	Legal	12	800	9.6
	Child care/wk	4	100	0.4
	..... Other	—	—	—
Structures:	Residential	4	240,000	960.0
	Commercial	2	340,000	680.0
	..... Other	—	—	—

GDP in current dollars **$19,027.6**

(B) Real or Constant GDP (in chained 2009 dollars):

Annual Domestic Output		Quantity in Millions	2009 Dollars	Value in Billions of $
Goods:	Automobiles	10	$25,000	$125.0
	Chairs	8	25	0.2
	..... Other	—	—	—
Services:	Legal	12	412	4.9
	Child care/wk	4	50	0.2
	..... Other	—	—	—
Structures:	Residential	4	114,740	459.0
	Commercial	2	69,469	138.9
	..... Other	—	—	—

GDP in constant dollars **$16,861.6**

for that matter. If real GDP, or GDP in constant dollars, changed by 2 or 3 percent, the difference *must* be due to changes in the number of goods, services, and/or structures produced after compensating for changes in price levels. The change *cannot* be due to inflation.

An additional advantage of using "real" terms is that only the percentage change is relevant, not the dollar or index value of the series. And, when we focus on percentage changes, the choice of the base year is not important.

GDP—A Measure of Output or Welfare?

Occasionally GDP is criticized on the grounds that it does not adequately measure our welfare, or our overall feeling of well-being.

So, do increases in GDP mean that we are really better off one might ask—especially during times of urban sprawl, environmental decline, congested traffic, high divorce rates, crime, and so on?[11] The short answer is that no single series could ever be comprehensive enough to take into account all of the factors that make us happy or unhappy. However, there is some truth to the assertion that GDP is at least a partial measure of welfare.

Let's see why!

We say this because a market economy is based on voluntary transactions. For example, whenever you buy something that was just produced (a transaction reflected in GDP), you must have felt that the money you gave up was worth less to you than the product you acquired—otherwise you would not have made the transaction. Likewise, the producer must have felt that the product given up was worth less than the money received—or the producer would not have made the sale. In the end, the exchange took place because both parties felt that they were better off after the transaction than they were before it took place. Because both parties were better off, there was an increase in welfare, even if we can't measure it!

Even so, we need to remember that GDP was designed as a measure of total output, not as an overall measure of welfare—so those who claim that it fails in this regard really miss the mark. The fact that GDP can tell us anything about welfare should be considered as a plus, and so we should be looking at the glass as if it were half full rather than half empty.

Does GDP Overlook Anything?

You bet! For example, GDP tells us nothing about the mix, or composition of output. A bigger real or constant dollar GDP only tells us that the dollar value of total output increased. We don't know if the increase was due to the production of new roads, homes, parks and libraries—or to the increased production of nerve gas, exotic military

---

[11] This argument is made by Cobb, Halstead, and Rowe, "If the GDP is Up, Why is America Down?" *Atlantic Monthly*, October, 1995.

defense expenditures, and toxic waste landfills. Also, GDP doesn't tell us anything about the quality of life. For example, you might feel that the quality of life is enhanced every time a new city park, swimming pool, or museum is built instead of nuclear weapons. Or, you might not.

Perhaps the biggest limitation is that GDP excludes nonmarket activities such as the services performed by homemakers and the services that people perform for themselves. For example, GDP will go down if a homeowner marries his or her housekeeper and does not hire a replacement. Likewise, GDP will go up if you hire someone to mow your own yard, but it will not go up if you do it yourself.

Other activities—prostitution, gambling, and drug running—are mostly illegal and are simply not reported to the IRS, Department of Commerce, or to anyone else. These activities are part of the underground economy and are not directly included in GDP, although estimates have been made for their inclusion.[12]

Gross National Happiness

Still, some people want to have a more comprehensive measure of welfare or happiness, and so we take note here of the official efforts made by the government of Bhutan to establish a measure of Gross National Happiness (GNH), which they prefer to GDP.[13] While their statistics are still in the early stages of development, they cover many traditional economic measures such as household income and home ownership along with many other noneconomic variables. For example, one of the components of GNH is the frequency of meditation (psychological wellbeing), another is the perception of soil erosion and river pollution (ecology), and yet another is long-term disability status and body mass indices (health).

Other components of GNH include the "ability to understand Lozey"—a rich oral poetic composition tradition—and "Zorig chusum skills"—the thirteen visual arts that the Bhutanese have practiced for generations. These components are culturally biased, of course, and

---

[12] In December 1985, GNP statistics extending back to 1929 were revised upward to account for the unreported underground economy activity. As a result of the revision, GNP in 1984 went up by $119.9 billion, and these revisions are now part of GDP. Even so, some private sector economists think that these revisions were not large enough.

[13] The websites at www.grossnationalhappiness.com report on these efforts. GNH is reported on a scale from 0 to 1, with a score of 1.0 being perfect happiness.

that makes international comparisons of GNH difficult, but they seem to work for the Bhutanese, which is why the GNH statistics were established in the first place.

One of the Great Inventions of the 20th Century

As you can tell by now, economists are passionate about their work, and they are passionate about their statistics—especially GDP and the national income and product accounts (NIPA) that support it. This endeavor is truly one of the remarkable efforts of our time, and the recognition the U.S. Department of Commerce bestowed on these efforts by announcing GDP as being "One of the Great Inventions of the 20th Century" is truly well deserved.[14]

Gross Domestic Product	
Compiled by:	Bureau of Economic Analysis in the U.S. Department of Commerce
Frequency:	Quarterly with two subsequent monthly revisions
Release date:	*Advance* estimate at the end of the first month following end of the quarter
Revisions:	*Second* estimate the end of the second month; *Third* revision at the end of the third month following end of the quarter; *Annual* revision every July; *Comprehensive* benchmark revision every 5 years
Internet:	http://www.bea.gov/ http://EconSources.com

---

[14] "GDP: One of the Great Inventions of the 20th Century," From the January 2000 Survey of Current Business, https://www.bea.gov/scb/account_articles/general/0100od/maintext.htm.

Recession vs. Depression

We generally want to know more than the size of GDP at any given time—we also want to see how it changes over time. The reason is that GDP does not always go up—it sometimes goes down as it did during the Great Recession of 2008–09.

Over time, most economists usually call successive contractions and expansions of GDP *business cycles*—which implies systematic changes in real GDP marked by alternating periods of expansion and contraction. Other economists prefer to talk of *business fluctuations*, which imply alternating, but not systematic, periods of contraction and expansion. Neither is perfect, but they both get the idea across.

When Is the Economy in a Recession?

That depends on the measure as two different definitions are used to address this question.

For example, the first definition has a recession occurring whenever real GDP (or GDP measured in constant dollars) declines for two consecutive quarters. This definition is popular because GDP is reported on a regular basis and it is fairly easy to keep track of changes in the quarterly GDP estimates.

The second—and ultimately official—definition is not from the Bureau of Economic Analysis, the Department of Commerce, or any other government agency. Instead, it comes from the National Bureau of Economic Research (NBER), a prestigious private institute with a long and distinguished record of research into the causes and measurement of business cycles.[15] According to the NBER, a recession is defined as "a significant decline in economic activity spread across the economy, lasting more than a few months, normally visible in real GDP, real income, employment, industrial production, and wholesale-retail sales."[16] When shown graphically in Figure 2-2,

---

[15]A list of the prominent economists who make up the NBER's business cycle dating committee can be found at http://www.nber.org. Also see "Determination of the December 2007 Peak in Economic Activity" article at the NBER site (December 11, 2008) for more on this topic.

[16] "The NBER's Recession Dating Procedure," January 7, 2008, http://www.nber.org

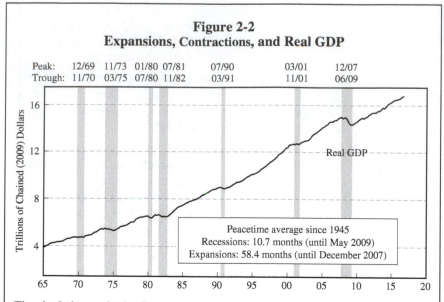

Figure 2-2
Expansions, Contractions, and Real GDP

Peak: 12/69 11/73 01/80 07/81   07/90   03/01   12/07
Trough: 11/70 03/75 07/80 11/82   03/91   11/01   06/09

Real GDP

Peacetime average since 1945
Recessions: 10.7 months (until May 2009)
Expansions: 58.4 months (until December 2007)

The shaded areas in the figure represent recessions which can be of varying durations. According to the NBER, the economy entered the last recession in December 2007 and did not begin to recover until the middle of 2009. This made the Great Recession of 2008–09 the deepest and longest recession since the Great Depression of the 1930s.

recessions appear shaded and the expansions are unshaded. Together, a recession and an expansion make up a business cycle.

To nail down the turning points of the business cycle, the NBER considers as much data as it can—most of it monthly—and then identifies specific months (rather than quarters) when the economy reached a relative peak or trough in economic activity. As a result, the NBER turning points may not always coincide with quarterly changes in real GDP. However, the prestige of the NBER is such that virtually all economists use the two-quarter definition of a recession only until the NBER announces the "official" business cycle turning points, which are shown in Table 2-3.

An advantage of the NBER approach is that monthly data are subject to less frequent revision than are the GDP numbers compiled by the BEA. A disadvantage is that many months may pass before the NBER makes an official announcement. For example, the NBER

Table 2-3
Business Cycle Expansions and Contractions in the United States

Peak	Trough	Peak	Recession	Expansion	Cycle
			Duration in Months*		

Peak	Trough	Peak	Recession	Expansion	Cycle
June 1857	December 1858	October 1860	18	22	40
October 1860	June 1861	April 1865	8	*46*	*54*
April 1865	December 1867	June 1869	*32*	18	*50*
June 1869	December 1870	October 1873	18	34	52
October 1873	March 1879	March 1882	65	36	101
March 1882	May 1885	March 1887	38	22	60
March 1887	April 1888	July 1890	13	27	40
July 1890	May 1891	January 1893	10	20	30
January 1893	June 1894	December 1895	17	18	35
December 1895	June 1897	June 1899	18	24	42
June 1899	December 1900	September 1902	18	21	39
September 1902	August 1904	May 1907	23	33	56
May 1907	June 1908	January 1910	13	19	32
January 1910	January 1912	January 1913	24	12	36
January 1913	December 1914	August 1918	23	*44*	*67*
August 1918	March 1919	January 1920	*7*	10	*17*
January 1920	July 1921	May 1923	18	22	40
May 1923	July 1924	October 1926	14	27	41
October 1926	November 1927	August 1929	13	21	34
August 1929	March 1933	May 1937	43	50	93
May 1937	June 1938	February 1945	13	*80*	*93*
February 1945	October 1945	November 1948	*8*	37	*45*
November 1948	October 1949	July 1953	11	*45*	*56*
July 1953	May 1954	August 1957	*10*	39	*49*
August 1957	April 1958	April 1960	8	24	32
April 1960	February 1961	December 1969	10	*106*	*116*
December 1969	November 1970	November 1973	*11*	36	*47*
November 1973	March 1975	January 1980	16	58	74
January 1980	July 1980	July 1981	6	12	18
July 1981	November 1982	July 1990	16	92	108
July 1990	March 1991	March 2001	8	120	128
March 2001	November 2001	December 2007	8	73	81
December 2007	June 2009	—	18	—	—
Averages for all cycles:					
	1854–2009 (33 cycles)		17.5	38.7	56.2
	1854–1919 (16 cycles)		21.6	26.6	48.2
	1919–1945 (6 cycles)		18.2	35.0	53.2
	1945–2009 (11 cycles)		11.1	58.4	69.5

*Cycles are measured from peak-to-peak; the underscored figures are for wartime periods.
Source: National Bureau of Economic Research and the *Survey of Current Business.*

took 8 months to declare that the 2001 recession had begun, and then another 20 months to decide that it was officially over. It also took 11 months for the NBER to decide that the economy had entered a recession in December 2007. Delays like this are partially responsible for the popularity of the first definition, especially when we are eager to know more about the current state of the economy.

What About a Depression?

It's difficult to give an exact definition of a depression because the U.S. economy experienced only one since 1865, and that was the Great Depression that began with the stock market crash in October of 1929 and lasted 43 months, or about 3½ years. Various estimates put the decline in real GDP by 40–50 percent although we have no way of knowing the exact decline because GDP had not yet been invented.

Even so, the extent of decline in the 1930s was extraordinary, and recessions both before and after never reached the extremes of production decline, joblessness, and price deflation that we experienced in the 1930s. Many modern contractions, with the exception of the Great Recession of 2008–09, were so mild that real GDP barely seemed to have declined at all, despite all of the attention paid to them in the media. Even the Great Recession was only 18 months long.

And yet our fascination with economic statistics remains undiminished as we are always interested in how long an expansion will last or when the next recession will take place. History is not always bound to repeat itself, but it can be a reasonably good guide to the future. For example, the second-longest expansion since the 1930s was 106 months under President Ronald Reagan while the longest one was 120 months under President Bill Clinton.

When this little book went to press in October 2017, the current expansion was exactly 100 months long. So, is a recession imminent, or can we break the 106 or 120 month records? We'll soon find out!

The NIPAs

The National Income and Product Accounts, or NIPAs, are a comprehensive set of nearly 300 accounts that provide detailed information on our nation's income and output. GDP is the best-known NIPA measure and is treated as the sum of the final expenditures of four sectors—consumers, private businesses, government, and a conceptual "rest of the world" sector to capture the net exports of and goods and services.

The approach of dividing the economy into sectors and then aggregating the sectors to get GDP is evident in Table 2-4 which presents the second estimate for the 2017-I quarter. The table also shows the size of each component in both current and constant (2009) dollar amounts, as well as their relative percentage sizes.

Are Other Statistics Related to GDP?

Good question! In fact, the very structure of the NIPAs almost guarantees that the majority of economic statistics are related to GDP one way or another. Some statistics report on the major components of total output like personal consumption expenditures or gross private domestic investment. Others track subcategories like durable and nondurable goods, and even others track the production of various product categories like automobiles and residential housing.

Many statistics, including most of those examined in this book, are designed to track GDP or one of its major components, while other statistics are designed to help predict future changes in the level of GDP or one of its major components. In addition, whenever anything is produced for the market, income is generated in the form of wages, tips, salaries, interest, rents, or profits. Since the recipients eventually spend this income, even more statistics are kept on these activities. Almost every economic statistic, then, is related to GDP in one way or another.

If there is a difficulty with most NIPA tables, it is that the numbers are so large as to boggle the mind. As a result, the BEA also presents another useful table that shows the contribution to the change in real GDP made by individual GDP components.

Table 2-4
The National Income and Product Accounts
First Quarter 2017 Second Estimate—Billions of Dollars

	Current	Constant (2009$)	% GDP
Gross domestic product	*$19,027.6*	*$16,861.6*	*100.0*
Personal consumption expenditures	*13,108.4*	*11,688.5*	*68.9*
Durable goods	1,439.1	1,642.4	7.6
Nondurable goods	2,779.5	2,530.6	14.6
Services	8,889.8	7,567.8	46.7
Gross private domestic investment	*3,149.1*	*2,902.2*	*16.6*
Fixed investment	3,147.4	2,879.0	16.5
Nonresidential	2,395.5	2,257.2	12.6
Structures	537.3	471.7	2.8
Equipment	1,074.3	1,055.4	5.6
Intellectual property	783.9	732.0	4.1
Residential	751.8	615.5	4.0
Change in private inventories	1.7	4.3	0.0
Net exports of goods and services	*(557.9)*	*(599.9)*	*(2.9)*
Exports	2,314.0	2,168.0	12.2
Imports	2,871.9	2,767.9	15.1
Government consumption and gross investment	*3,328.0*	*2,899.3*	*17.5*
Federal	1,260.4	1,115.2	6.6
National defense	732.1	656.2	3.8
Nondefense	528.2	458.0	2.8
State and local	2,067.7	1,782.3	10.9
Residual		*(57.8)*	

Source: Tables 1.1.5 and 1.1.6, second estimate, Bureau of Economic Analysis. The first column of numbers shows current dollar entries, the second column shows "real" or constant dollar entries that are based on the chain weighting calculations discussed the Appendix. Also, note that one of the idiosyncrasies of chain weighting is that "real" or constant dollar amounts are sometimes larger, and sometimes smaller, than their corresponding current dollar amounts—as a result, a residual is employed because chain weighted numbers cannot be added. The percent of GDP column is based on current dollars; percentages are slightly different for chain weighted dollars.

Table 2-5 shows the contributions to percent changes in real GDP for four consecutive quarters. The most recent quarter in the table shows annualized first-quarter growth at 1.2 percent. The biggest contribution came from gross private domestic investment at 0.78 percent while the weakest contribution came from government consumption and gross investment at a −0.20 percent.

Table 2-5
Contributions to Percent Change in Real GDP
Percent Change at Annual Rates—First Quarter 2017 Estimate

	2016-II	2016-III	2016-IV	2017-I
Gross domestic product	*1.4*	*3.5*	*2.1*	*1.2*
Personal consumption expenditures	*2.88*	*2.03*	*2.40*	*0.44*
Durable goods	0.70	0.84	0.82	−0.11
Nondurable goods	0.80	−0.07	0.47	0.18
Services	1.37	1.26	1.11	0.37
Gross private domestic investment	*−1.34*	*0.50*	*1.47*	*0.78*
Fixed investment	−0.18	0.02	0.46	1.85
Nonresidential	0.12	0.18	0.11	1.34
Structures	−0.06	0.30	−0.05	0.69
Equipment	−0.17	−0.26	0.11	0.39
Intellectual property	0.35	0.13	0.05	0.27
Residential	−0.31	−0.16	0.35	0.50
Change in private inventories	−1.16	0.49	1.01	−1.07
Net exports of goods and services	*0.18*	*0.85*	*−1.82*	*0.13*
Exports	0.21	1.16	−0.55	0.69
Imports	−0.03	−0.31	−1.27	−0.55
Government consumption & gross investment	*−0.30*	*0.14*	*0.03*	*−0.20*
Federal	−0.02	0.16	−0.08	−0.14
National defense	−0.13	0.08	−0.14	−0.16
Nondefense	0.10	0.08	0.06	0.02
State and local	−0.28	−0.02	0.11	−0.06

Source: Table 1.1.2, first quarter second GDP estimate, Bureau of Economic Analysis.

The advantage of the table is that it helps us see some of the emerging strengths and weaknesses of the economy. For example, it is clear that the decline in personal consumption expenditures from the fourth quarter of 2016 was largely due to the decline in durable goods spending which went from 0.82 and −0.11, while the change in private inventories of −1.07 was a major drag on gross private domestic investment. There's a lot in the table that we can't hope to explain right now, we just want to show its value as a tool to uncover potential problem areas in the economy.

Personal Income

Personal income sounds as if it should be about the income people earn: their salaries, tips, and hourly wages. In a way it is, but in a more fundamental sense, ***personal income (PI)*** represents the total current income received by persons from all sources *minus* social insurance payments. A more direct measure is **disposable personal income (DPI)**, the amount we have left to spend after taxes and non-tax payments.

GDP may be the primary measure of the nation's total output, but it is not the best measure of the nation's income for two reasons. First, GDP *includes* output generated with resources owned by foreign residents. Since income earned by these individuals leaves the United States, it cannot be included as part of our nation's income. Second, GDP *ignores* income earned by U.S. residents as a result of their investments abroad.

Table 2-6 shows the two adjustments necessary to convert GDP (the measure of total domestic output) to GNP (the measure of total domestic income).[17] The first step is to add the income earned by U.S. residents as a result of their international investments. The second step is to subtract the income earned by foreign residents as a result of their investments in the United States. Because it usually takes longer to get some of this information, estimates of GNP always lag GDP estimates.

Table 2-6
Converting GDP to GNP, Billions of Current Dollars

Gross domestic product (GDP)	**$19,027.6**
Plus: Income receipts earned abroad	883.9
Less: Income payments to foreign residents	646.8
Gross national product (GNP)	**19,264.8**

Data are for 2017-I second estimate, Table 1.7.5, Bureau of Economic Analysis

---

[17] In the case of the United States, the two adjustments are nearly offsetting, so that GNP and GDP are almost the same. This is not always the case for other countries. Canada's GDP is usually several percentage points larger than its GNP because foreign investments in Canada are much larger than Canadian investments in the rest of the world.

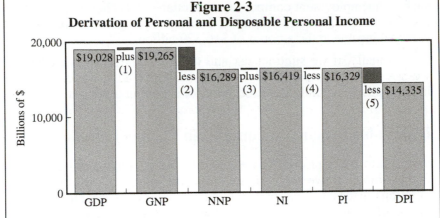

Figure 2-3
Derivation of Personal and Disposable Personal Income

Note: data are annualized 2017-I estimates
(1) Factor income payments to foreigners are subtracted, and factor income receipts from foreign residents are added to GDP to get gross national product (GNP).
(2) Consumption of fixed capital is subtracted from GNP to get net national product (NNP).
(3) A statistical discrepancy is added to equate NNP and national income (NI).
(4) Undistributed corporate profits, corporate income taxes, and social insurance contributions are subtracted and transfer payments are added to NI to get personal income (PI).
(5) Tax and nontax payments are subtracted from PI to get disposable personal income (DPI).

The rest of the NIPA components are shown in Figure 2-3. To go from GNP of $19,264.8 billion to a *net national product* (*NNP*) of $16,289 billion, we subtract the wear and tear on the capital stock, more formally known as *consumption of fixed capital.* The BEA then needs a modest statistical discrepancy to arrive at the measure called *national income (NI)* of $16,419 billion.[18] NI represents the sum of employee compensation, proprietors' income, rental income, corporate profits, and net interest payments in the economy.

To get to *personal income* (*PI*), undistributed corporate profits (retained earnings) and contributions for social insurance payments like

---

[18] The BEA uses two ways to estimate GDP in the NIPAs, one is through an incomes approach and the other is through an expenditures approach. The statistical discrepancy is used to rectify the difference between the two as they seldom match.

social security are subtracted. At the same time, transfer payments, such as unemployment compensation, welfare, and other aid, are added in. The result, shown in Figure 2-3, is the aggregate measure called personal income in the amount of $16,329 billion.

Finally, if we subtract tax and other nontax payments from PI, we get ***disposable personal income (DPI)*** of $14,335 billion, the income people actually have left over for spending purposes.

Disposable Personal Income as an Economic Indicator

Before we plot DPI, we should note its remarkable stability. For example, if we were to examine the nominal (unadjusted for inflation) disposable personal income series from 1965 until 2017, a period of 52 years or 208 quarters, we would find that it only turned down a total of eight times—and four of those declines were during the Great Recession of 2008–09. When measured in constant or real dollars, the series shows a bit more instability, but not much.

Figure 2-4 shows DPI in both nominal and real (2009) dollars from 1965 until the first quarter of 2017.[19] Overall both series rise modestly during expansions and are relatively flat to negative during recessions. In retrospect, this is exactly the pattern we should have expected. DPI is such a large component of GDP, about 75 percent, that both should to go up and down together even though the quarterly movements are relatively small. In fact, DPI would have been down a little more during the recessions had it not been for transfer payments that act as buffers to lessen the decline.

On rare occasions DPI can even be affected by political events. Right after the presidential election of 1992, many individuals who feared higher tax rates under the Clinton administration arranged to have their annual bonuses paid in December of 1992, rather than wait for January when a new tax year—and possibly higher tax rates— would apply.[20] This spike in the data has since been removed, but it's entirely possible for it to happen again.

---

[19] Personal income data are collected and published both monthly and quarterly. The monthly data are released in BEA's "Personal Income and Outlays" news release. Quarterly estimates for personal income are published in the *Survey of Current Business* along with other NIPA accounts.

[20] Under the Clinton administration, Congress made the individual income tax more progressive by adding a fourth marginal tax bracket of 39.6 percent which applied to taxable income over $250,000.

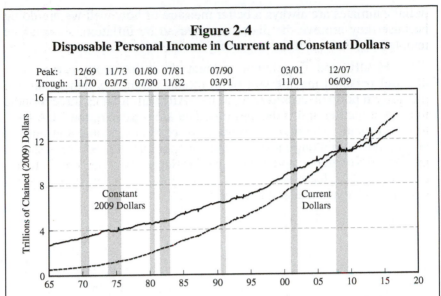

Figure 2-4
Disposable Personal Income in Current and Constant Dollars

Disposable personal income is fairly stable and often goes up even during most recessions, although the Great Recession of 2008–09 is an exception because of its severity. The constant dollar measure is preferred by economists, although the current dollar measure is the one most frequently reported in the press.

What Else Should We Know About Personal Income?

First, because PI and DPI are such large and relatively constant components of GDP, they behave more as coincident indicators than as leading or lagging ones. Coincident indicators don't give us the advance warning of where the economy is heading that leading indicators do, but they are nevertheless important because they tell us where we are and how well we are doing.

Also, we should note that because personal income is one of the major NIPA components, it is subject to the same revisions as GDP. This means that any new announcement of personal income will almost always mention a revision of the previous monthly or quarterly figures.

While the BEA releases both real (chained 2009 dollars) and current dollar estimates simultaneously, the press often seems to focus on the current dollar figures because the amounts are larger. But, real dollar estimates are always a better measure of how well we are doing because they remove the distortions caused by inflation, so don't be tempted to just look at the largest figures.

Finally, the first announcement we hear about personal or disposal personal income will be in monthly numbers rather than the quarterly reports discussed here so far. After all, it takes three months to make a quarter and if the monthly data are available, the BEA likes to report them. The monthly release for personal income and outlays also comes with a one month delay; for example, a report released on the 1st of November will have data for September, but not October. Each monthly release also comes with a full list of interesting tables which provide a considerable level of detail.

Personal and Disposable Personal Income

Indicator status:	Coincident economic indicator overall
Compiled by:	Bureau of Economic Analysis
Frequency:	Monthly
Release date:	beginning of month
Revisions:	Second and third revisions of the advance estimates
Published data:	*Economic Indicators*, Council of Economic Advisors
	Survey of Current Business, U.S. Department of Commerce
	Personal Income and Outlays, BEA News Release, U.S. Department of Commerce
Internet:	http://www.bea.gov
	http://www.EconSources.com

Chapter 3

PRODUCTION and GROWTH

Purchasing Managers' Index

Economists have long been interested in predicting the output of goods, and one of the more interesting indicators of this activity is the monthly *Purchasing Managers' Index* (*PMI*) compiled by the Institute for Supply Management (ISM).[1] The series is reliable as both a *coincident* and a *leading* indicator—meaning that it tells us where the economy is and where it is likely to be going. It is one of a handful of major series maintained by a private industry and/or educational group rather than a division in the U.S. Department of Commerce.[2]

The PMI is the major component of the ISM's monthly Report on Business which surveys manufacturing firms on a number of topics including production, new orders, inventories of purchased materials, employment, prices, backlog of orders, and supplier deliveries. The ISM releases the PMI on the first business day following the close of the reporting month. Its usefulness and accessibility makes it a perennial favorite among economic forecasters.

---

[1] ISM, formerly known as the National Association of Purchasing Management (NAPM), is a not-for-profit association that exists to educate, develop, and advance the purchasing and supply management profession. With more than 50,000 members, ISM and its affiliates in 90 countries work to establish and maintain best-in-class professional standards pertaining to research, education, and certification.

[2] Other series examined in this book include, but are not limited to, the *Help-wanted Advertising Index* and the *Consumer Confidence Survey* compiled by The Conference Board, the *Index of Consumer Expectations* compiled by the Institute for Social Research at the University of Michigan, the *Dow Jones Industrial Average* compiled by the Dow Jones Corporation, and the *S&P 500* by Standard & Poor's Corporation.

The Sample and the Survey

The PMI is derived from a monthly survey of purchasing managers at hundreds of companies in 18 manufacturing industries. Each industry is weighted according to its contribution to GDP, and each firm in the industry is given equal weight, regardless of its size.[3] The questions, similar to the following example, are designed to detect changes in the direction and intensity of business activity[4]:

> SUPPLIER DELIVERIES - Check the **ONE** box that best expresses the current month's **OVERALL** delivery performance compared to the previous month.
>
> ☐ **Faster** than   ☐ **Same** as a   ☐ **Slower** than
>   a month ago   month ago   a month ago

When all of the responses are collected, the results are tabulated and then reported in the form of a diffusion index.

What Does a Diffusion Index Tell Us?

A diffusion index is different from other series in that it focuses on the direction and magnitude of change as opposed to the absolute level of the series. The diffusion index used by the ISM ranges from 0 to 100 percent and is considered to be expanding whenever it has a value greater than 50 percent, so the more the number exceeds 50 percent, the more intense the expansion of the series. By the same token, the series is contracting when the index is less than 50 percent—and the smaller the number, the more intense the contraction.

In addition to the series on supplier deliveries, separate indices are constructed for production, new orders, inventories of purchased materials, customers' inventories, employment, prices, backlog of orders, new export orders, and, imports. These 10 series are combined to make up the overall Purchasing Managers' Index.

---

[3] Bretz, Robert J., "Behind the Economic Indicators of the NAPM Report on Business," July 1990, in NAPM's *Report on Business Information Kit*, March 2000.

[4] To illustrate, weights of 1, 0.5, and 0 are given to each of the three responses. If half of the respondents select "faster" and if half respond "slower," the index will have a value of 50 percent [or, $0.5(1) + 0.5(0) = 0.5$]. Likewise, if 60 percent respond "faster," 20 percent "same," and 20 percent "slower," the index will have a value of 70 percent [or, $0.6(1) + 0.2(0.5) + 0.2(0) = 0.7$].

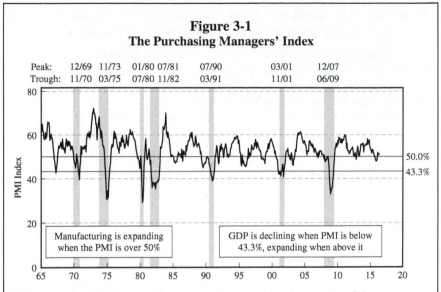

Figure 3-1
The Purchasing Managers' Index

Whenever the PMI is over 50 percent, the manufacturing sector of the economy is expanding. Whenever the PMI is greater than 43.3 percent, the overall economy—which includes services in addition to manufactured goods—is expanding. Because the PMI is a diffusion index, it has the properties of a leading indicator, reaching a peak before the economy peaks and a trough before the economy reaches a trough.

The Historical Record

Figure 3-1 shows the PMI since 1965. The manufacturing sector of the economy is claimed to be generally expanding when the index is above 50 percent, and contracting when below that level. The horizontal line at 43.3 percent is the value of the index thought to be most consistent with no change in real GDP, so the overall economy should be expanding when the PMI is above 43.3, and contracting when the index is below it.[5]

It also helps to examine the intensity and direction of change as well as the general level of the index. For example, when the index was above 43.3 percent and *rising,* the economy was indeed

---

[5] This number is revised annually because GDP is continually being revised. When the last edition of this book was published in 2010, the number was 41.2 rather than 43.3. However, most PMI changes are relatively small, in the range of one or two tenths of a percent annually.

expanding. Yet, when the index was above 43.3 and *declining,* the economy was beginning to slow and headed for a recession.[6]

The reason for this is that the PMI is a diffusion index, which means that it also has the properties of a leading indicator. If we examine Figure 3-1, we can see that the index peaked, with highly variable lead times, well in advance of every recession. Likewise, the index usually hits a minimum just before the recovery began.[7]

Purchasing Managers' Index	
Indicator status:	The level of the PMI is a *coincident* indicator; peaks and troughs in the PMI function more as *leading* indicators with highly variable lead times
Compiled by:	Institute for Supply Management (ISM)
Frequency:	Monthly
Release date:	First business day following close of the reporting month
Revisions:	None, responses are raw data and are not changed
Published data:	*Manufacturing Report On Business*, ISM's monthly publication
Internet:	www.ismrob.org

---

[6] A 1985 paper presented by Theodore S. Torda at the NAPM International Conference and later published in *Purchasing Management* (July 1985, pp. 20–22) states that ". . . monthly data on the NAPM composite index and the Commerce Department's composite of leading economic indicators . . . (both) tend to reach their peaks and troughs before those of the general business cycle." Later in the same paper, the author states that "the NAPM composite index clearly leads the (BEA) coincident index."

Another paper by Alan Raedels, "Forecasting the NAPM Purchasing Managers' Index," in the *Journal of Purchasing and Materials Management* (Fall 1990), concluded that "the PMI can be considered a coincident indicator of the economy."

[7] A peak in the series is analogous to an inflection point in a series that grows first at an increasing and then at a decreasing rate. The trough is analogous to an inflection point for a series that decreases at an increasing and then at a decreasing rate.

Index of Industrial Production

The *index of industrial production* is a comprehensive index of industrial activity compiled by the Board of Governors of the Federal Reserve System. Because of the Fed's responsibility for monetary policy, and because of delays in reporting final GDP, the index is designed to give the Fed a quicker reading on the overall health and activity of the manufacturing sector of the economy.

The overall index is made up of approximately 300 individual series that represent a broad range of industries. The data are collected directly from numerous sources, including gas and electric utilities, the Bureau of Mines, the Census Bureau, other government agencies, and industry trade associations.[8] After the source data are compiled and weighted according to their respective industry size, they are expressed as a percentage of base-year output with monthly estimates released mid-month of the following month.[9]

Industrial Production and GDP

Industrial production covers the goods portion of GDP and amounts to about 22 percent of total output. The Industrial Production series is reported several ways: the first is the *total* index, which is a compilation of all individual indices; a second tracks durable and nondurable consumer goods production; a third features major market groups—with subcategories for consumer goods, business equipment, information processing, national defense and space equipment, construction and business supplies. Finally, a fourth tracks major industry groups to highlight activity in the manufacturing, mining, and utilities industries. These reports are all possible because the nearly 300 individual series can be grouped in a variety of different ways.

---

[8] Oddly enough, the Fed uses some quarterly series to compile the monthly index of industrial production. The Fed does this by making monthly estimates that are then revised as the quarterly data become available.

[9] The industrial production index represent the level of real output relative to the current base year of 2012. The monthly production index is anchored to annual benchmarks that, according to the Fed, "are less timely but typically based on more comprehensive data." See "Technical Aspects of the Revision," *Annual Revision, Industrial Production and Capacity Utilization—G.17*, March 31, 2017.

What About the Historical Record?

Figure 3-2 shows that the total index of industrial production usually behaves as a coincident indicator, meaning that the peaks and troughs in the series occur at approximately the same time that the economy has its peaks and troughs. This is to be expected, since overall industrial production represents such a large proportion of total GDP.

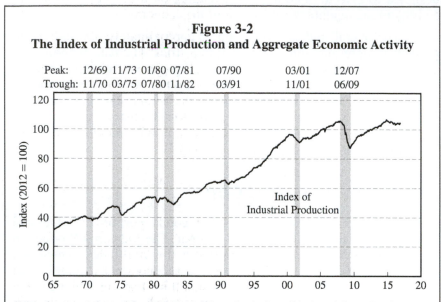

Figure 3-2
The Index of Industrial Production and Aggregate Economic Activity

Peak: 12/69 11/73 01/80 07/81   07/90   03/01   12/07
Trough: 11/70 03/75 07/80 11/82   03/91   11/01   06/09

With the exception of the 2001 recession, the index of industrial production normally behaves as a coincident indicator, with changes in the series normally taking place at about the same time as changes in the direction of overall economic activity. The severity of the 2008–09 Great Recession was such that the index fell by more than 20 percent, taking it back to a level of activity recorded ten years earlier in mid-1998.

When the durable and nondurable goods series are presented separately, as shown in Figure 3-3, it is evident that the durable goods portion of the index is the more volatile component. This normally occurs because the purchase of durable goods—automobiles, boats, furniture, and appliances that last more than three years under normal conditions—can usually be postponed if consumers find themselves short of purchasing power.

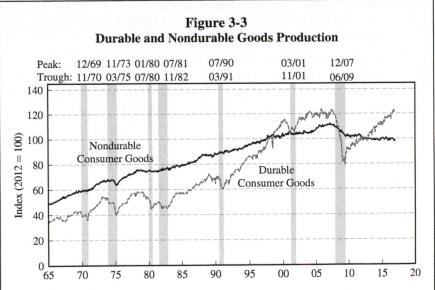

Figure 3-3
Durable and Nondurable Goods Production

The durable goods component of the industrial production index is more volatile than for nondurables. The durables index also performs better as a leading indicator for recessions because it usually reaches a peak just before a recession begins, and then begins to recover just before the recession ends.

Monthly Estimates and Revisions

The initial release of the index of industrial production, like most other economic data, is subject to considerable revision. The process is complicated by the fact that the overall index is made up of so many different series, most of which become available at separate times, and some of which are themselves subject to further monthly revisions.

The Fed deals with this problem by substituting its own estimates for missing data if data have not yet been received.[10] To illustrate, if electric power usage data are not available when the initial report is issued, the Fed makes a judgment as to what it thinks the numbers should be. The same is done for other missing data, so a

---

[10] See Charles Gilbert, Norman Morin, and Richard Raddock, "Industrial Production and Capacity Utilization: Recent Developments and the 1999 Revision," *Federal Reserve Bulletin*, March 2000.

portion of the initial release is based on the Fed's estimates. Then, as better data become available over the next three to five months, it is used in place of the Fed's estimates.

Despite these procedures, the initial release is fairly reliable. As for revisions, whenever the Fed releases the latest industrial production number for the month, it shows both the preliminary and the revised estimates for the preceding five months.

Index of Industrial Production

Indicator status:	Overall index generally coincident with changes in real GDP, although the durable goods component is more of a leading indicator for recessions and recoveries
Compiled by:	Federal Reserve System Board of Governors
Frequency:	Monthly
Release date:	Preliminary estimate around the fifteenth of the following month
Revisions:	Preliminary estimate subject to revision in each of the subsequent 5 months and annual revisions every spring
Published data:	*Economic Indicators*, Council of Economic Advisors *Statistical Release G.17*, Federal Reserve System
Internet:	https://www.federalreserve.gov/releases/g17/Current/ http://www.EconSources.com

Capacity Utilization

When the Federal Reserve System collects data on industrial production, it also makes estimates of manufacturing capacity. When the Fed compares the level of industrial production to manufacturing capacity, the result is *capacity utilization*. This monthly series is generally regarded as being a leading economic indicator for downturns in overall economic activity.

Measuring Capacity Utilization

The Fed's data on manufacturing capacity, like its *index of industrial production*, are expressed in terms of an index with a base year of 2012 = 100. The two are then divided to express production as a percentage of actual capacity:

$$\text{Capacity Utilization} = \frac{\text{Index of Industrial Production}}{\text{Index of Industrial Capacity}}$$

In February 2017, for example, the industrial production index stood at 103.7 while the capacity index stood at 136.7. When the former was divided by the latter, capacity utilization was 0.759 or 75.9 percent.

Estimates of industrial capacity are available for a number of industries and product groups including manufacturing, mining, utilities, durable goods, chemicals, and paper, to name a few. The monthly series is released approximately two weeks after the close of the month and is closely watched by many economists, especially those who watch the Fed.

Why Is Capacity Important to the Fed?

One of the responsibilities of the Fed is to foster steady economic growth in a climate of reasonable price stability. The capacity utilization rate is designed to tell the Fed if the economy is "heating up" to the point where inflation might surge because of production bottlenecks. This sometimes happens when demand for output is so strong that producers are tempted to use less skilled labor and less efficient equipment to generate even more output.

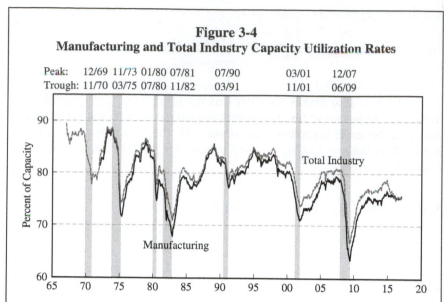

Figure 3-4
Manufacturing and Total Industry Capacity Utilization Rates

Peak: 12/69 11/73 01/80 07/81   07/90   03/01   12/07
Trough: 11/70 03/75 07/80 11/82   03/91   11/01   06/09

Originally, the Fed made capacity utilization estimates for manufacturing. It later added mining, utilities, and several others to get a "total industry" series which are now available from 1967 to the present. Despite the availability of several separate "total" series, manufacturing gets most of the attention—even though the two series behave about the same.

When the capacity utilization rate gets high, the Fed might be tempted to tighten the money supply to slow the economy and lessen the threat of inflation. When the capacity utilization rate is low, the economy is perceived to have some "slack" that acts to ease inflationary pressures.

What About the Historical Record?

The capacity utilization rates for two series, manufacturing and total industry, are shown in Figure 3-4. Because the series are expressed as a percent of total capacity, their levels never exceed 100. Historically, the Bureau of Economic Analysis classified both as leading indicators for peaks in real GDP, although the lead times are too variable to be of precise value for forecasting.

The capacity utilization series, like most other economic data, is continually revised as new information becomes available and modifications in data collection and processing are introduced. Because capacity utilization is a ratio of two other series, a revision of either affects the ratio. Consequently, the monthly numbers are revised for up to five additional months, and the entire series is revised every spring.

This series is a little different from our other economic indicators in that it is not exclusively intended to forecast changes in future economic activity—but is instead designed as an aid to monetary policy.

Capacity Utilization	
Indicator status:	Leading for recessions; coincident for recoveries
Compiled by:	Federal Reserve System Board of Governors
Frequency:	Monthly
Release date:	Preliminary estimate made midmonth of following month
Revisions:	The preliminary estimate is revised for up to 5 months; annual revisions every spring
Published data:	*Economic Indicators*, Council of Economic Advisors
	Statistical Release G.17, Fed Board of Governors
Internet:	https://www.federalreserve.gov/releases/g17/Current/
	http://www.EconSources.com

Labor Productivity

A key measure of efficiency in the U.S. economy is *output per hour of all persons*, more commonly known as **labor productivity**. This is a quarterly statistic published by the Bureau of Labor Statistics and is important because labor productivity is a key component of long-term economic growth.

Several labor productivity series are released simultaneously in the quarterly BLS *Productivity and Costs* report. One covers the non-farm business sector, another the business sector, and a third manufacturing—with both durable and nondurable components.[11] Labor productivity is compiled using monthly, quarterly, and even annual data that are subject to frequent revision. As a result, there can be some variation in the numbers reported for any given quarter.

How Do We Measure Productivity?

The official BLS definition of business or labor productivity is as follows:

$$\text{Productivity} = \frac{\text{Index of real dollar output}}{\text{Hours of labor input}}$$

The numerator is based on, but is not exactly identical to, the GDP statistics in the national income and product accounts.[12] To prevent prices from distorting the dollar value of the numerator, it is measured in real terms. The denominator is obtained from the BLS Current Employment Statistics (CES) program that provides monthly employment data on payrolls in various industries.[13]

While a seemingly simple measure, labor productivity is affected by many non-labor factors such as changes in technology, capital investments, and managerial skills—all of which affect the numerator, the index of real dollar output.

---

[11] In March 2017, the BLS released the 2016 fourth quarter productivity report of 1.3 percent for the nonfarm business sector, 2.0 percent for the business sector, and 2.0 percent for the manufacturing sector.

[12] For example, outputs of government, nonprofit institutions, paid employees of private households, and rental value of owner-occupied dwellings are all excluded.

[13] *BLS Handbook of Methods,* Chapter 10.

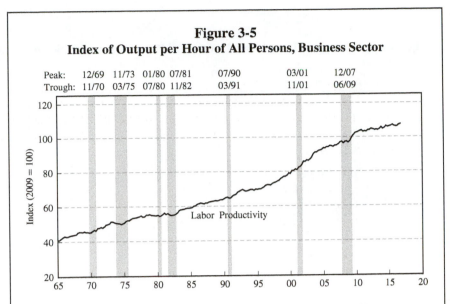

Figure 3-5
Index of Output per Hour of All Persons, Business Sector

Peak:	12/69	11/73	01/80	07/81	07/90	03/01	12/07
Trough:	11/70	03/75	07/80	11/82	03/91	11/01	06/09

Labor productivity is defined as the amount of constant or real dollar output produced per hour of labor input. Labor productivity is an important component of economic growth, but as a quarterly report it is not well suited for short-term forecasting purposes.

The Historical Record

The historical series shown in Figure 3-5 indicates that total business sector productivity grew modestly from the mid-1960s until the mid-1990s. The growth rate then increased until the Great Recession, and then tapered off again. The index reached 107.1 in the first quarter of 2017, meaning that workers produced 7.1 percent more output per hour than they did in 2009. The productivity rate for the manufacturing sector (not shown) during the same quarter was 119.2, or 19.2 percent higher than in 2009.

Business sector labor productivity exhibits modest cyclical behavior as it declines just before or during most recessions. Economists think this may occur because employers tend to hire less skilled, and therefore less productive, workers when production is high and unemployment rates are low. These workers are also the first to be laid off during a recession, which explains the resurgent productivity growth at the end of most recessions.

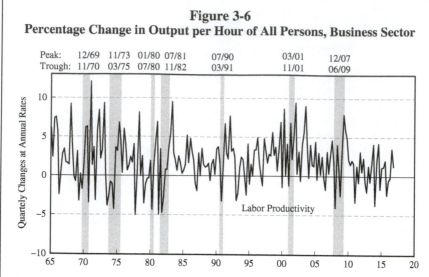

Figure 3-6
Percentage Change in Output per Hour of All Persons, Business Sector

Quarterly changes in labor productivity can be quite dramatic from one quarter to the next. Productivity figures are best thought of as being related to long-term growth; they are unrelated to the turning points in the overall level of economic activity.

When labor productivity is expressed as a percentage change from the preceding quarter, as shown in Figure 3-6, it is evident that quarter-to-quarter changes are both volatile and generally unrelated to turning points in real GDP. As a result, changes in business sector labor productivity have little value as indicators of short-term future economic activity.

Multifactor Productivity

A drawback of labor productivity is that it does not include contributions made by other factors of production such as capital and technology. This is why many economists attribute the spurt in productivity growth during the latter half of the 1990s to the widespread use of the personal computer rather than just labor.

Accordingly, several *multifactor productivity* measures have been developed which incorporate a combination of inputs such as labor, capital, energy, and other resources. Unfortunately, some of the source data needed to construct these measures are not available quarterly, so the series are only compiled annually. However, annual data are not very useful for forecasting purposes as there were only six declines in the 30 years since the series began in 1987—and two of them occurred during the Great Recession of 2008–09.[14]

Labor Productivity in Perspective

Labor productivity is useful when we want to explain factors that contribute to long-term economic growth. However, these measures ignore changes in the use of other inputs like computers, energy, and other factors of production. Consequently, any change in the quantity or quality of other resources can make labor seem as if it is more productive than it really is.

Productivity numbers are slow to be reported because they are constructed using so many different annual, quarterly, and monthly series, data which must first be generated in order for productivity to be computed. Finally, the historical record shows that quarterly productivity numbers have little value as a forecasting tool.

None of this is intended to disparage labor productivity, of course, but we do need to know how the series is measured and behaves if we are to interpret and use it properly.

Labor Productivity	
Indicator status:	None
Compiled by:	Bureau of Labor Statistics
Frequency:	Quarterly
Release date:	About 40 days after the close of the quarter
Revisions:	First revisions 30 days after the initial release, additional revision 60 days after initial release
Published data:	*Monthly Labor Review*, U.S. Department of Labor *Economic Indicators*, Council of Economic Advisors
Internet:	https://www.bls.gov/lpc/ http://www.EconSources.com

---

[14] The other four annual declines were in 1991, 1993, 1995, and 2016. See Table 3. "Private nonfarm business sector, indexes of productivity and related measures, 1987-2016," on the BLS multifactor productivity website at http://www.bls.gov/mfp/.

Leading Economic Index

One of the most useful statistical series is the *Leading Economic Index (LEI)*, a monthly series designed to tell us where the economy is headed. The LEI is released by The Conference Board (TCB) at the beginning of every month and is calculated from a variety of private and government series released during the previous month.[15] Essentially, the series is a predictive tool to tell us if, and approximately when, a recession might take place. It is one of the most closely watched indicators of future economic activity.

How Was the Leading Index Developed?

Intuitively, the concept of a leading indicator is fairly easy to grasp. We start with the observation that the overall economy is made up of all types of economic activity. Next we ask, could it be that some activities take place or that some events occur in *advance* of changes in the overall economy? If so, perhaps we could focus on these activities and use them to predict how the entire economy might behave in the near future.

Back in the 1950s, the National Bureau of Economic Research (NBER) thought this might be happening so they compared thousands of statistical series to changes in real GNP. One set of data examined was an index of stock market prices, which, as it turned out, usually declined sharply just before a recession got underway.

Theoretically, the linkage between stock prices and overall spending makes sense. For example, if people feel poorer because of their losses in the market, they might decide to cut back on spending. If enough people feel poorer, their collective decision to spend less may actually affect economic growth.

By itself, however, a measure of stock price performance could not be used as the sole indicator of future economic activity because

---

[15] The series was compiled by the U.S. Department of Commerce for almost 30 years, but was transferred to The Conference Board in December of 1995 as part of a federal budget saving measure. The Conference Board is a private, not-for-profit, non advocacy organization that publishes several other statistical series including the *Help-wanted Advertising, Consumer Confidence*, and *Business Confidence* indices.

stock prices sometimes went down while the economy went up. Using the approach that there is safety in numbers, why not look for other statistical series to combine with stock prices?

It turned out that building permits for private housing also behaved somewhat like stock prices—with the total number of permits issued tending to decrease several months before the economy turned down. Again, this seems to make sense because a decline in building permits may well mean that a substantial amount of economic activity will either be delayed or not take place at all.

Eventually, the list was narrowed down to a handful and then combined to form a composite index. The resulting series usually changed direction some months *before* the economy did, hence the term "leading indicator." The index offered considerable promise, so the Department of Commerce took over the task of collecting and publishing the data. Eventually, responsibility for compiling the series was transferred to The Conference Board, making the composite index in Table 3-1 the first-ever privatization of an official U.S. government statistical series.[16]

Table 3-1
Components of the Leading Economic Index

1. Average weekly hours, manufacturing
2. Average weekly initial claims for unemployment insurance
3. Manufacturers' new orders, consumer goods and materials
4. ISM new orders index for manufacturing
5. Manufacturers' new orders, nondefense capital goods excl. aircraft
6. Building permits, new private housing units
7. Stock prices, 500 common stocks
8. The Conference Board's Leading Credit Index
9. Interest rate spread, 10-year Treasury bonds less federal funds
10. Consumer expectations for business conditions (University of Michigan series)

Source: The Conference Board, March 2017

How Do We Interpret the Index?

In general, most observers focus on changes in the direction and duration of the index to forecast an upcoming recession. For

---

[16] Monthly LEI updates and working papers that describe comprehensive benchmark revisions to the U.S. series can be found on The Conference Board's website at https://www.conference-board.org/data/.

example, if the index declines for three consecutive months, it is often thought that the leading index has signaled that a recession is about to begin.

In the same way, three consecutive monthly increases are often taken as a sign that the economy will soon begin to prosper or continue to prosper. The most difficult case to interpret is one where the index goes up for several months and then down for several months—or moves in no particular pattern as it sometimes does when the economy is weak or a turning point is near.

The Historical Record

Figure 3-7 shows the leading index along with shaded areas that represent recessions so that we can compare the index turning points with real GDP contractions. According to the figure, every recession since 1965 was preceded by a significant drop in the LEI. The recession warnings given by the index ranged from as few as 8 to as many as 21 months, with a 13.3 month average.

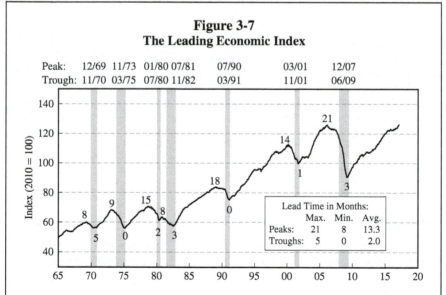

Figure 3-7
The Leading Economic Index

Peak:	12/69	11/73	01/80 07/81	07/90	03/01	12/07	
Trough:	11/70	03/75	07/80 11/82	03/91	11/01	06/09	

Lead Time in Months:

	Max.	Min.	Avg.
Peaks:	21	8	13.3
Troughs:	5	0	2.0

The Leading Economic Index (LEI) predicted the Great Recession of 2008–09 by 21 months. In addition, previous recessions were also predicted by significant lead times according to the most recently revised TCB series.

Less important, but worth mentioning, is the ability of the index to predict when a recession is about to end. Figure 3-7 shows that the lead time warnings ranged from 0 to 5 months, with 2.0 being the average. However, because it takes several months or more to recognize a turning point in the index, the economy is usually well out of the recession before the index signals its prediction.

Most of the early controversy concerning the index focused on whether or not three consecutive downturns actually forecast an economic slowdown. Specifically, the index showed several consecutive months of decline in 1966, 1984, and 1995 even though a downturn never occurred.

Did The Conference Board's Revisions Help?

Economists think so. In fact, the revisions resulted in three improvements. First, the size of the "false signal" in 1984 was muted. Second, the size of the 1989 downturn was more pronounced, giving a stronger warning of the impending recession. Third, the size of the false signal given in 1995 was reduced, even though the index showed a significant pause.

On the other hand, the historical data for the TCB's revised series still showed a false warning for mid-1966. Other revisions, such as the change to a newer base year, had no bearing on the turning points of the series. Overall, however, the LEI certainly performed well enough when it predicted the Great Recession that began on December 2007 and lasted through June 2009, so it seems to be on track.

Has the Index Ever *Failed* to Predict a Recession?

No, but it has predicted some recessions that never occurred!

The first was in 1966 when the index declined for nine consecutive months while the economy continued to grow. However, heavy—and to some extent hidden—spending on the Vietnam War may have provided enough stimuli to avoid a recession.[17]

---

[17] Economic expansions and/or contractions are sometimes excluded during wartime periods because of the distortions caused to real GDP.

Another false prediction occurred in March 1984 when the index turned down for seven consecutive months. Again, however, massive federal deficit spending—to the tune of $200 billion annually in 1985 and 1986—seems to have helped the economy avoid a recession. Finally, a series of declines in early 1995 presented another puzzling period for the leading index. At the time, it seemed the index had peaked, but strong economic growth in 1996 seemed to pull the index up again.

So, the short answer to our question is this: the LEI has predicted every recession since 1965—along with a few others that never occurred. These false predictions were substantially muted after The Conference Board's revisions, but they were never fully erased. And, while revisions to the index will most likely improve future forecasts, they weren't of any help when the past problems occurred.

Are There Other Problems with the Index?

Frequent revisions of the monthly numbers can be a major source of frustration. For example, whenever a new monthly LEI number is announced, revisions are sometimes made to previous LEIs if revisions were made to any of the underlying components.

Suppose we have a period when the index has already turned down two months in a row. We anxiously await the next report and it turns out to be another decline, but is coupled with an upward revision of an earlier (negative) monthly number. This leaves us back where we started, with two *newer* consecutive months of decline—and our attention again riveted on the coming month's LEI.

In addition, some observers follow changes in the 10 components of the LEI in hopes that they can forecast the change in the index before the new monthly LEI is actually announced. After all, the general direction of the leading index is usually known before the official number is released. This gives rise to an oft-heard statement that "Economists forecast an 'xx' percentage change in the LEI when it comes out tomorrow." This type of forecast really doesn't help anyone because it causes people to think that one or the other—the economists or the LEI—don't know how to get it right.

Despite some of these minor issues, the Conference Board's improvements have made the LEI a useful and popular forecasting device. The peaks in the series are more distinct, and the lead times are more consistent. This makes it is one of the main tools in the forecaster's tool kit, and one of the most-watched statistical series in the economy today.

Leading Economic Index	
Indicator status:	Leading for recessions and recoveries
Compiled by:	The Conference Board
Frequency:	Monthly
Release date:	About 4 weeks after the close of the reporting month
Revisions:	Up to six previous months are revised with every new release
Published data:	*Business Cycle Indicators,* The Conference Board
Internet:	http://www.conference-board.org/

Preface: Data, Information, Understanding, Wisdom

Seven years have passed since the last edition of this little Guide was published. During that time, we came off a period of substantial if imperfect economic success and then fell into the infamous Great Recession, so called to remind us of how close it came to the disastrous Great Depression of the 1930s. We have since experienced—and apparently are continuing to experience—a slow and uneven climb to improved production and growth. And all the while we see our world and our economy undergoing remarkable technological, geo-political, social, and environmental transformations.

Among the most remarkable of these transformations, and the most relevant to our Guide, is the enormous and rapid increase in the digital data churned out by all of our various activities. Google, Facebook, Wikipedia, customer loyalty cards, telephone, Internet, and credit and debit card records, etc. are just the visible surface of this vast and growing pool of data.

But data, by themselves, tell us very little. They are the inert building blocks of concepts yet to be imagined and yet to be built. This is where our economic statistics come in. Compiling, analyzing, and distilling these building blocks into coherent statements are the tasks to which our statistical indicators are dedicated. And in doing so, they turn data into information.

Information, of course, is what we want to have. It tells us where we have been and where we might be going and helps us make important personal, family, and business decisions. Our wallets, our "breadbaskets," our careers are influenced by these decision making tools. To ignore them would be like flying blind or driving cross country without a GPS or without even a road map: not impossible perhaps, but not advisable.

Good information like good statistics, tends to come as a flow over time. Our statistics are constantly evolving. They are regularly updated. The samples on which some of them are based, such as the market basket of consumer goods and services from which the Consumer Price Index is calculated, are adjusted to reflect changing consumer buying behavior. The sets of statistical series included in various indices are similarly adjusted to our changing economic structure. And other technical, methodological, and definitional revisions are made to increase the accuracy of the economic information they provide.

It is only natural that some statistics take on more importance—and others less so—as time goes on. The political responses to our recent economic difficulties have made government fiscal policies—government expenditures and taxes—more important than they have been for several decades. International investment and trade have also become bigger issues during that time. Economic statistics reporting on these newer concerns have moved closer to center stage.

Accessibility to our economic information also continues to evolve. Thirty years ago, many of the individual series that were used to keep track of the economy were available on the ECONOMIC BULLETIN BOARD of the U.S. Department of Commerce for a relatively modest fee. In 1995, as part of a cost-saving measure some of the most important business cycle series were transferred to The Conference Board, a private, non-profit business organization, which sold them to users at a significantly higher cost. Since then, most federal information generating agencies have put their series on the internet, thereby increasing accessibility and lowering the cost to users. Most of the federal sites now also have utilities that allow users to retrieve a staggering amount of information in a wide variety of formats. And always, easy access to much of this is provided by www.EconSources.com.

Finally, the public media seems to have a voracious appetite for numbers. Press releases from private and public statistical sources are picked up and quoted virtually verbatim, as if they were doctrine from on high. We are left to sort it out. That is, we are left to transform information into understanding. Here is where our little book becomes especially important. It has no axe to grind. It is neither a statistics lecture nor an economics textbook. Instead, it is a handy little guide that can be consulted for clarification whenever any of the statistical series dealt with herein are encountered. It examines how different series are constructed and how we may use them effectively. Above all, it tries to put this information in context, so the reader can see how the economic statistics lead to an understanding of the larger picture.

Chapter 4

INVESTMENT and CAPITAL EXPENDITURES

Gross Private Domestic Investment

One of the four main sectors of the economy is investment spending by businesses, a category officially known as **gross private domestic investment**. This category includes a number of expenditures, but residential and nonresidential spending on structures, equipment, and intellectual property are the main ones.

Gross private domestic investment is currently the third largest of the four main NIPA categories, but it only accounts for less than 17 percent of GDP. This may not seem like much, so why should we be so interested in this component of GDP? The answer is rooted in the long search for stable and predictable economic relationships.

The Search for Stable Relationships

When John Maynard Keynes wrote his magnificent *General Theory of Employment, Interest, and Money* during the Great Depression of the 1930s, he offered a bold and radical explanation of how the economy functioned.[1] His approach was based on a conceptual framework that divided the economy into sectors and then described, in considerable detail, the spending behavior of each.

Keynes argued that spending by consumers, the largest of his four main sectors, was relatively stable. This was important because

---

[1] John Maynard Keynes, *The General Theory of Employment, Interest, and Money*, Harcourt, Brace & Co., New York, 1936.

if the greatest part of the economy was relatively stable and predictable, then instability of the whole economy must be due to another—a smaller and more volatile—component. He then argued that spending by the business, or the investment, sector was likely to be the least stable.

Despite the fact that there were no existing GDP statistics that could be used to verify his convictions, Keynes' description of spending by each sector—consumer, business, government, and the international or foreign sector—was so detailed that academicians had to collect and then analyze reams of data to test his theories. In the end, research largely confirmed the propositions put forth in *The General Theory*. Before long, the data grew into the NIPA accounts that feature the GDP, GNP, NNP, and other measures of aggregate economic performance that we use today.[2] The organization of Tables 2-4, 2-5, 4-1, and numerous other tables and figures used throughout this book, are directly influenced by Keynes' work.

Table 4-1 presents the economy's four main sectors following the format of Table 2-4, only this time the focus is on quarterly GDP percentage changes that have taken place since 1965. The first column shows the relative spending for each category in the first quarter of 2017—with the consumer sector accounting for 68.9 percent of total expenditures, the government sector accounting for 17.5 percent, the businesses sector accounting for 16.6 percent, and the foreign sector with −2.9 percent. Columns 2 and 3 show the maximum and minimum percentage changes, and the mean percentage change is shown in the fourth column. The coefficient of variation (CV), a measure of relative stability, appears in the last column.[3]

Even the most casual inspection of the table reveals the stability of the consumer sector and the relative instability of the investment, or

---

[2] Simon Kuznets, the second American to win the Nobel Prize in economics, was already working on a set of national income accounts when Keynes wrote *The General Theory*. His data were used to test some of Keynes' theories.

[3] The coefficient of variation (CV) is the standard deviation divided by the mean, a measure that allows us to compare the variability of two series with different means. To illustrate, the CV of 0.5 for personal consumption expenditures tells us that quarterly percentage changes for this sector are one of the most stable in the table. A CV of 2.4 for gross private domestic investment means that quarterly percentage changes in this series are roughly 4.8 times (or 2.4/.5) more volatile than personal consumption expenditures.

Table 4-1
Quarterly Percentage Changes in GDP Components, 1965–2017

	% of GDP in 2017-I	Maximum Change	Minimum Change	Mean Change	CV
Gross domestic product	*100.0*	*5.8%*	*(2.0%)*	*1.6%*	*0.6*
*Personal consumption expenditures**	*68.9*	*4.2%*	*(2.6%)*	*1.7%*	*0.5*
Durable goods	7.5	12.4%	(8.7%)	1.5%	1.9
Nondurable goods	14.6	4.4%	(7.5%)	1.4%	0.9
Services	46.7	4.4%	(0.6%)	1.8%	0.4
Gross private domestic investment†	*16.6*	*13.6%*	*(13.2%)*	*1.6%*	*2.4*
Fixed investment	16.5	9.0%	(8.3%)	1.6%	1.4
Nonresidential	12.5	9.5%	(7.8%)	1.7%	1.3
Residential	4.0	17.9%	(16.6%)	1.6%	2.9
Change in private inventories	0.0	—	—	—	—
Net exports of goods and services‡	*(2.9)*	—	—	—	—
Exports	12.2	22.5%	(11.2%)	2.1%	1.8
Import	15.5	20.3%	(17.2%)	2.3%	1.8
Govt. purchases of goods, services§	*17.5*	*4.6%*	*(1.1%)*	*1.5%*	*0.8*
Federal	6.6	6.1%	(4.2%)	1.3%	1.4
State and local	10.9	5.0%	(0.9%)	1.7%	0.7

*Consumer sector   †Business sector   §Government sector   ‡Foreign Sector

gross private domestic investment sector, that was predicted by Keynes.[4] This instability should be enough to make it worthy of study—but there's more. Investment sector expenditures, Keynes argued, have a way of causing *additional* expenditures through the multiplier principle.[5]

The multiplier is defined as the change in overall spending caused by a change in investment spending—and the multiplier works in both directions. On one hand, a reduction of investment spending by businesses would translate into an even larger reduction in overall spending, which Keynes felt was largely responsible for the Great Depression of the 1930s. On the other hand, "pump priming" in the form of additional government spending would have the opposite

[4] Because the change in private inventories is such a small component of GDP, and because the net foreign sector was much smaller and less significant when Keynes published *The General Theory* in 1936, we did not compute CVs for either.
[5] The President's Council of Economic Advisors has estimated that the multiplier for the United States economy is about 2. This means that $1 billion of investment spending will ultimately generate about $2 billion of spending on total output.

impact—that of causing even more spending in hopes that it would
put the economy back on track to recovery and growth.

Figure 4-1 gives us a visual feel for the relative instability of
gross private domestic investment sector spending—an instability that
is further magnified by the presence of the multiplier. The 2.4 CV
value in Table 4-1 is further evidence of the historical instability of
this sector's spending.

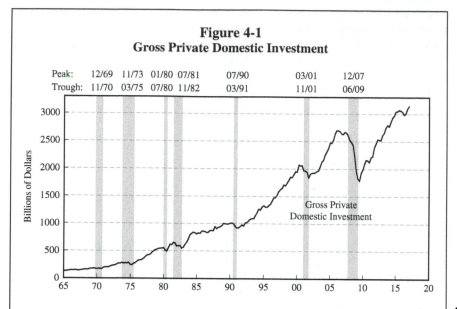

Figure 4-1
Gross Private Domestic Investment

Peak:	12/69 11/73 01/80 07/81	07/90	03/01	12/07
Trough:	11/70 03/75 07/80 11/82	03/91	11/01	06/09

Because of the multiplier effect, changes in *gross private domestic spending,*
spending that accounts for about 17 percent of total GDP spending, have a
magnified impact on overall economic activity because of the multiplier. The
multiplier for the U.S. economy has a value of about 2.

Declines in business investment sector spending are therefore
thought to be major factors associated with recessions. The decline
in business spending preceded the Great Recession of 2008–09 by
about 18 months. As for the other recessions in Figure 4-1, the
declines started much closer to, or just as, the recessions began. In
almost every case, however, investment spending continued to
decline for the duration of the recession. Clearly expenditures by
this sector warrant close attention if we are concerned about the
stability of GDP.

Looking Back—But Not Forward

At one time, the government kept a series on planned or new plant and equipment expenditures.[6] However, the level of planned plant and equipment expenditures did not track well with the actual, so it was dropped after the second quarter of 1994 in favor of a new semiannual series based on an Annual Capital Expenditures Survey (ACES).

Unfortunately, the ACES plans were then dropped for budgetary reasons even before any data were ever published. And so, despite the obvious importance of investment sector spending, and despite numerous series that track specific investment sector categories, the federal government currently has no forward-looking series regarding planned capital expenditures.

The reason we watch the *gross private domestic investment* series is that it helps explain some of the observed variations in real GDP. It also helps to see that it is becoming a more reliable leading economic indicator for recessions. The downside is that it, like many other NIPA components, is a quarterly report that often does a better job of telling us where we are, rather than where we are headed.

Gross Private Domestic Investment

Indicator status:	Leading indicator for recessions; coincident for recoveries
Compiled by:	Bureau of Economic Analysis
Frequency:	Quarterly
Release date:	End of the month with GDP revisions
Revisions:	Second, and third revisions of the advance estimate
Published data:	*Economic Indicators*, Council of Economic Advisors
	Survey of Current Business, U.S. Department of Commerce
Internet:	https://www.bea.gov/
	http://www.EconSources.com

---

[6] At the beginning of the year, firms would report their plans for first-quarter spending. If these plans were delayed, some respondents would simply push the planned expenditures ahead to the next quarter. Then, when the last quarter arrived, there was a tendency for firms to simply cancel the delayed expenditures altogether, thus causing distortions in the quarterly figures. To make matters worse, benchmark revisions that were normally done every 5 years or so to assure the validity of the sample were not conducted after 1982. As a result, the series became less and less reliable.

New Building Permits and Housing Starts

According to Table 2-5 on page 29, the growth of spending on residential construction was relatively tepid from 2016-II until 2017-I. Quarterly growth rates ranging from −0.31 to 0.50 percent may not seem like much, especially when total spending on residential construction is only 4.0 percent of GDP, but the problem is that the multiplier still magnifies their impact on the economy. Consequently several series are used to track housing activity, but the two that receive the most attention are the number of *new building permits* issued, and the number of *new housing starts*.[7]

The first series is formally known as *new privately-owned housing units authorized by permit-issuing places*—which explains its more common and considerably shorter title. This series is based on a monthly survey of 9000 permit-issuing places and is the only housing series included in The Conference Board's LEI although other series are available.[8] The second measure discussed here is *new privately-owned housing units started*. This differs from building permits in that it represents actual homebuilding activity, not just the *intention* to build. The Census Bureau releases both series mid-month following the close of the reference month.

Do Building Permits Predict Future Economic Activity?

On one level, the relationship between new building permits issued and overall economic activity may seem tenuous. After all, a building permit represents the intention to spend rather than actual spending. The intent to build may also be adversely affected by changes in interest rates after the permit is issued, or even changes in

---

[7] Two others are *real gross private residential fixed investment* in chained (2009) dollars and the Department of Housing and Urban Development's (HUD) *National Housing Market Summary*. The former tracks the housing component of the NIPA accounts and is reported quarterly. The latter is a quarterly report on U.S. national housing indicators, including series on the supply of and demand for housing.

[8] The preliminary release of *new building permits* on a seasonally adjusted annual basis is available on the twelfth workday of every month and is the one reported in the press. The final figures for the series are available on the eighteenth workday and are the ones included in TCB's *Leading Economic Index (LEI)*.

the builder's financial situation. As a result, the amount of time between issuance of the permit and the start of the new residence could vary significantly.

Finally, a building permit is also relatively inexpensive to obtain and is sometimes acquired partially for precautionary reasons—for example, "in case" the opportunity to build is right. In short, there are several reasons why the number of building permits issued might not work very well as an economic indicator.

What About Housing Starts?

This series is similar to building permits in that it is expressed in terms of thousands of private houses started annually. It also exhibits a high degree of volatility. To illustrate, housing starts fell by 9.6 percent in September 2016, rose by 25.5 percent in October, then dropped by 12.9 percent in November before it finally rose by 11.0 percent in December.

Weather is often the cause of such changes. Since permits are relatively inexpensive and easy to obtain, a builder may have a backlog of building permits and may be waiting for favorable weather to begin construction. Changing interest rates are another factor, especially when the Fed actively raises or lowers interest rates to control inflation or stimulate the economy. Finally, a builder usually waits for a customer to receive financing before a house is started.

The Historical Record

Collectively there may be several reasons as to why these series might not work very well when it comes to predicting future changes in overall economic activity.

But, work well they do. As can be seen in Figure 4-2, in most cases building permits and new housing starts tend to reach a relative peak before the economy enters a recession. Then, both series tend to rebound sharply during the recession, thereby announcing the impending arrival of the recovery.

A minor problem evident in Figure 4-2 is the volatility of the series. Monthly directional changes are not infrequent, and a large monthly change in one direction can be followed by a sharp reversal

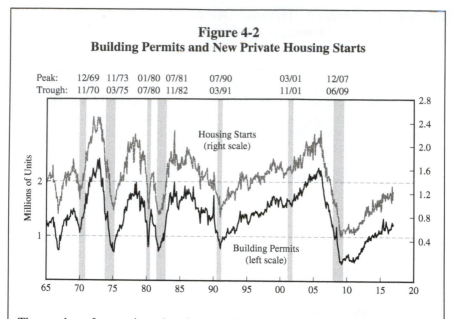

Figure 4-2
Building Permits and New Private Housing Starts

| Peak: | 12/69 | 11/73 | 01/80 | 07/81 | 07/90 | 03/01 | 12/07 |
| Trough: | 11/70 | 03/75 | 07/80 | 11/82 | 03/91 | 11/01 | 06/09 |

The number of new private housing permits issued and new private housing units started both function as leading indicators for recessions and recoveries. The main problem with both series is the relative size of the month-to-month variations which can obscure the underlying trend.

in the next. During 2016, a year in which real GDP showed modest but consistently positive economic growth, the building permits index changed direction four times, with a low of −7.3 percent in March and a high of 6.3 percent in September.

Some volatility is due to the nature of the series, but some is also due to sampling variability. For example, the Census Bureau uses a mail survey to collect building permit data from local building permit officials. When requested reports are not received, missing values are simply estimated and then revised later when the data are received.

Finally, the astute reader may have noticed that for any given year in Figure 4-2, it seems as if there are more housing starts than building permits issued. That in fact is the case, and it occurs because many unincorporated areas outside town or cities limits do not require building permits.

Is One Preferable to the Other?

Probably not. The good news is that both series function reasonably well as leading indicators for both peaks and troughs in overall economic activity. As for peaks, Figure 4-2 clearly shows severe and protracted drops in both series just before the recessionary periods. As for troughs, both series seem to recover before the economy begins to recover.

The bad news is that the volatility of both series often includes changes in the *direction* of movement as well as magnitude. As a result, the Census Bureau claims that "it may take three months to establish an underlying trend for building permit authorizations, six months for total starts, and six months for total completions."[9]

The main problem with both building permits and housing starts is one of interpretation as the focus often seems to be on the size of the preliminary monthly change rather than on the underlying trend. Because it takes a few months for the data to be revised and the trend established, we have to be patient and not put too much emphasis on the most recent monthly report.

Building Permits and Housing Starts	
Indicator status:	Both series, leading for recessions and recoveries
Compiled by:	Both, the Census Bureau
Frequency:	Monthly
Release date:	Preliminary (both series): twelfth workday of the month
	Final (both series): eighteenth workday of the month
Revisions:	Building permits: initial report revised twice monthly;
	Housing starts: initial report revised twice monthly
Published data:	*Monthly New Residential Construction*, U.S. Census Bureau, Department of Commerce
	Economic Indicators, Council of Economic Advisors
Internet:	https://www.census.gov/construction/nrc/index.html
	http://www.EconSources.com

---

[9] U.S. Census Bureau and the U.S. Department of Housing and Urban Development's *Monthly New Residential Construction, February 2017*. News Release, March 2017.

Business Inventories

Historically, inventories have played an important role in the literature on recessions and expansions.[10] While there are a number of series from which to choose, our most important aggregate is the ***total manufacturing and trade inventories*** series, more commonly called ***total business inventories***, which is compiled by the U.S. Census Bureau.[11]

In general, high levels of inventories have been singled out as contributing to the cause of recessions, while low inventory levels are sometimes thought to be a sign that business activity is about to pick up. To see how this might come about, let's take a simplistic look at the process.

How Do Inventory Levels Affect Economic Activity?

First, it helps to think of inventories as being a buffer between production and sales. Suppose, for example, that consumers suddenly and unexpectedly cut back on their spending. The result is likely to be rising levels of unsold business inventories in stores and warehouses. If businesses then reduce orders from suppliers, or close factories in order to reduce inventory levels, workers will either work shorter hours or lose their jobs.

This, in turn, reduces the amount of income workers have to spend, which may cause inventory levels to *increase*, rather than decrease, as businesses had planned. If the cycle repeats itself, production will again fall, unemployment will rise, and consumer spending will drop, all of which may put the economy firmly on the path to recession.

---

[10] W.S. Jevons, Wesley Mitchell, and John Maynard Keynes were but a few of the many economists to incorporate the role of inventories into their view of the causes and explanations of economic fluctuations. In the late 1940s, Moses Abramovitz's classic work, *The Role of Inventories in Business Cycles*, was published by the National Bureau of Economic Research and did much to influence the way inventory statistics are compiled and reported today.

[11] There is more than one inventory series from which to choose. The FRED Economic Data research site at the Federal Reserve Bank of St. Louis lists more than 1,300 series under the heading of "inventories." https://fred.stlouisfed.org.

Eventually businesses may succeed in reducing production to the point where inventories are too low. If they overshoot their mark, or if consumer spending increases even slightly, inventory shortages may develop. Businesses will then need to hire more instead of fewer workers. This increases employment and consumer spending, causing inventories to go down again rather than up. As long as businesses continue to try to replenish inventories, the process of playing catch-up helps pull the economy out of recession and put it on the path to recovery.

Does It Really Work Like That?

As can be seen in Figure 4-3, inventory levels of tend to rise during the latter part of an expansion and then turn down as, or shortly after, a recession begins—which makes the series a coincident or a lagging indicator for recessions. In fact, any series that reports on the *level* of inventories is usually more of a lagging indicator than a coincident one.

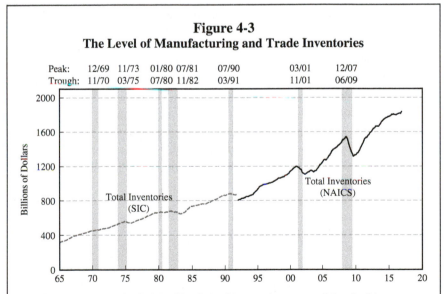

Figure 4-3
The Level of Manufacturing and Trade Inventories

Peak: 12/69 11/73 01/80 07/81   07/90   03/01   12/07
Trough: 11/70 03/75 07/80 11/82   03/91   11/01   06/09

Total Inventories (SIC)

Total Inventories (NAICS)

Monthly reports on the *level* of business inventories are useful coincident or lagging indicators for recessions, although they are of little value for predicting subsequent recoveries. Since 1982, all inventory data were valued on a current-cost basis, rather than at book values.

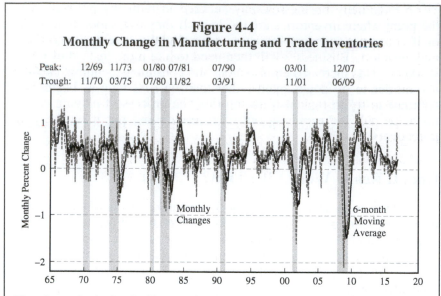

Figure 4-4
Monthly Change in Manufacturing and Trade Inventories

The *change* in the level of inventories rather than the *level* itself, behaves more like a leading indicator for recessions. But, because month-to-month fluctuations are so wide, a 6-month moving average is often used to smooth the series. Note that the series does not have to predict every recession in order to be classified as a leading indicator—it just has to work most of the time.

Of course there is always more than one way to look at data, so let's try again. This time, in Figure 4-4, we will look at the *change* in the level of inventories rather than at the level itself.

As for this new series, the monthly percentage change in the level trade inventories looks more like a leading indicator for recessions, with the series usually reaching a peak well before GDP turns down. The leading tendencies are more evident when a moving average is used to reduce the volatility, so this gives us yet another way to look at inventories as an economic indicator. As for recoveries, however, the monthly change series seems to behave as a coincident indicator.

So Why Bother with Inventory *Levels*?

Because others do! In fact, some financial writers insist on reporting the level of business inventories (or a given subset) even though it is not helpful as an indicator of future economic activity.

What Should We Remember About Inventory Statistics?

First, any series that reports on inventory levels tends to act as a coincident or lagging indicator for recessions. Second, if we look at changes in the level of inventories, the data behave more as leading indicators. Monthly percentage changes are highly variable, however, and so moving averages are often used to smooth the data.

Finally, as difficult as changes in monthly inventor levels are to interpret, they are nevertheless important because they are a small but important component of our GDP.

Business Inventories	
Indicator status:	Inventory levels are coincident or lagging indicators for recessions
	Changes in the level of inventories are usually leading indicators for recessions, coincident for recoveries
Compiled by:	Census Bureau
Frequency:	Monthly
Release date:	Three weeks after the close of the reference month
Revisions:	Preliminary estimate revised in subsequent month
Published data:	*Economic Indicators*, Council of Economic Advisors
	Manufacturing and Trade Inventories and Sales, U.S. Department of Commerce
Internet:	https://www.census.gov/mtis/index.html
	http://www.EconSources.com

Inventories/Sales Ratio

Inventories may be a relatively small part of the overall economic picture, but their volatility is such that they attract more than their fair share of attention. We can look at the level of inventories, the change in the level of inventories, or even use inventories as part of a ratio. The Census Bureau even compiles several ratios of inventories to sales, but the most comprehensive is the monthly **total business inventories/sales ratio** that appears approximately six weeks following the close of the reference month.

Advantages of Ratios

Among the several advantages of ratios, two stand out. First, ratios can be constructed from other statistical series without actually having to collect new data. Second, ratios allow us to observe the interaction between two related series—inventories and sales in this case.

A third advantage here might be that a ratio using the absolute levels of inventories and sales is likely to be less volatile than monthly percentage changes in the levels of either. Consequently, a ratio might even be a good indication that something important is likely to happen.

Leading Indicator Status

The proof of the pudding, it is often said, "is in the eating"—or in Figure 4-5 to be more exact. Specifically, the inventory to sales ratio in the figure is far more stable than the monthly percentage changes in inventory levels shown in Figure 4-4 on page 68.

Overall, and with the exception of the Great Recession of 2008–09, the ratio has behaved fairly well as a leading indicator for recessions by turning up well before the recession arrives. Perhaps the failure to worsen (i.e., turn up) prior to 2008 was an aberration, but it certainly stands out as a departure from the historical trend that began in the early 1990s.

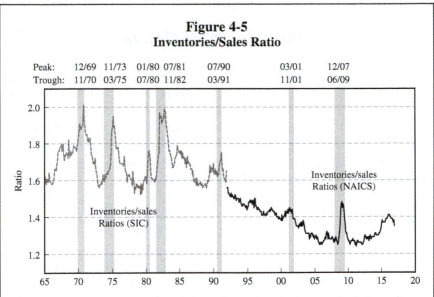

Figure 4-5
Inventories/Sales Ratio

Peak:	12/69	11/73	01/80	07/81	07/90	03/01	12/07
Trough:	11/70	03/75	07/80	11/82	03/91	11/01	06/09

With the exception of the 2008–09 Great Recession, the inventories/sales ratio
was useful because it turned up just before a recession began, making it a possible
leading indicator of future economic downturns. Because it is a ratio, month-
to-month changes are considerably smaller than changes to just the numerator
by itself.

The aberration in 2008 is also a reminder that we can never rely
exclusively on a single measure to determine the economy's current or
future health. This is why economists always like to analyze changes
in other data to provide cross validation.

Inventories/Sales Ratio	
Indicator status:	Historical leading economic indicator for recessions
Compiled by:	Census Bureau
Frequency:	Monthly
Release date:	Mid-month following the reference month
Revisions:	Approximately 10 days after the initial mid-month release
Published data:	*Manufacturing and Trade Inventories and Sales*, U.S. Department of Commerce
Internet:	https://www.census.gov/mtis/index.html
	http://www.EconSources.com

Durable Goods Orders

Durable goods, goods that last at least three years under normal use, constitute a significant part of aggregate economic production. The consumer sector's 7.5 percent of durable goods spending in Table 4-1 is only part of the story as total durable goods production for all sectors was closer to 18 percent of total output.[12]

A reliable monthly measure that tracks this component of GDP is ***manufacturers' new orders: durable goods***. It is compiled from surveys of approximately 4300 reporting units from about two-thirds of the manufacturing companies with $500 million or more of shipments that were reported in the most recent Economic Census.[13]

The historical series of manufacturers' new orders of durable goods is shown in Figure 4-6. It is widely watched because new durable goods orders usually decline sharply either before or at the onset of a recession.

How Do Durable Goods *Orders* Differ from *Production*?

One difference is that the Census Bureau collects data on durable goods orders and reports the results in billions of dollars, whereas the Fed's series on durable consumer goods production is reported in the form of an index.[14]

Another difference is in the relative timing of the two series. Because some durable goods are usually ordered before they are produced, it would seem as if the series on durable goods orders would provide an earlier warning of an impending recession. Indeed, this seems to be the case although the peaks in both series are relatively close.

---

[12] *Table 1.2.6. Real Gross Domestic Product by Major Type of Product*, National Income and Product Accounts, Bureau of Economic Analysis.

[13] The durable goods order series is published in the *Monthly Advance Report on Manufacturers' Shipments, Inventories and Orders*. The sample is from the 2012 Economic Census and is updated in 5-year intervals.

[14] The Fed's monthly *Index of Industrial Production* was illustrated earlier in Figure 3-2 on page 40.

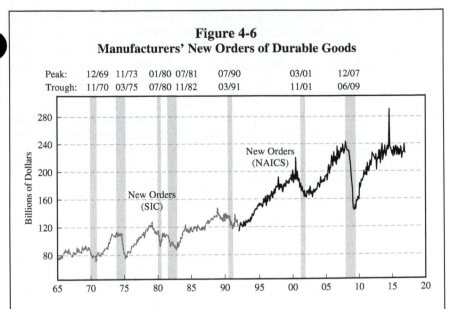

Figure 4-6
Manufacturers' New Orders of Durable Goods

Peak:	12/69	11/73	01/80 07/81	07/90		03/01	12/07	
Trough:	11/70	03/75	07/80 11/82	03/91		11/01	06/09	

New orders for durable goods may have leading indicator status, but the monthly numbers are so volatile that it is sometimes difficult to identify relative peaks and troughs. For the NAICS series shown in this figure, there were 144 monthly declines and 156 monthly increases—an almost a perfect balance between the number of increases and decreases.

However, the main difference is in the volatility of the two series. Whereas the *production* of durable consumer goods increased by about 40% between June 2009 and early 2017, manufacturers' *new orders* of durable goods increased by almost 60% over the same period. The same is true for most other periods, with new orders being more volital than production.

Just How Useful Is the Series?

Historically, the new orders series gave a decent performance as a leading indicator for recessions even though it is fairly volatile from one month to the next. In fact, since 1992 the series turned down about as often as it turned up, even though there were many more years of economic expansion than recessionary ones.

In addition to these frequent changes of direction, some of the monthly changes were quite dramatic. For example, in July 2014, new orders for durable goods rose 23.0 percent only to decrease by 18.4 percent the very next month. Whenever a statistical series exhibits this much volatility, it is difficult to infer much from any given monthly change. Instead, it is usually better to use a moving average to smooth out the short-term changes, although this is currently not done.

Unfortunately a large change in any statistical series usually captures the attention of the press, and too much is often made of it. This is especially true when most of the other economic indicators are giving mixed signals—a combination of events that encourages people to look for more significance in a monthly report than is really warranted.

Even so, the new durable goods orders series has historically performed well as a leading indicator for recessions because it tends to peak before or just as the economy peaks. It also tends to bottom out at, or sometimes slightly after, the economy bottoms out which makes it more of a coincident indicator for recoveries. However, the variability of the lead times, along with the number and size of the monthly changes, means that any new monthly report of this indicator should be interpreted with caution.

Durable Goods Orders

Indicator status:	Leading indicator for recessions, coincident for recoveries
Compiled by:	Census Bureau
Frequency:	Monthly
Release date:	Advance report about 18 working days after the end of the reference month
Revisions:	Regular report about 23 working days after end of month; annual revisions every spring
Published data:	*Economic Indicators*, Council of Economic Advisors
	Monthly Advance Report on Manufacturers' Shipments, Inventories and Orders, U.S. Census Bureau
Internet:	https://www.census.gov/economic-indicators/
	http://www.EconSources.com

Chapter 5

EMPLOYMENT and UNEMPLOYMENT

Total Employment

Numbers on employment and earnings are important to all of us. At a personal level, being employed means that we can take home a paycheck, and that's something that is near and dear to most of us. At the macroeconomic level, changes in the total number of people employed tell us a lot about the state of the economy. Even the National Bureau of Economic Research (NBER) uses the total employment situation to help establish the beginning and ending dates of a recession, and The Conference Board uses some of the BLS employment data in its monthly *Leading Economic Index.*[1]

While several statistical series would allow us to follow employment trends, perhaps the most popular is the **total nonfarm payroll employment** series that is released monthly by the Bureau of Labor Statistics.

Collecting Employment Statistics

Every month, state agencies use a national survey provided by the BLS to collect monthly data on employment, hours, and earnings from approximately 147,000 businesses establishments and government agencies that represent approximately 634,000 workers. This effort is known as the "establishment survey" and its data are the featured component of the *Current Employment Statistics* (CES) program.

---

[1] See pages 23–26 for the NBER business cycle dating procedure; page 51 for the individual components of The Conference Board's *Leading Economic Index.*

Because only business and government establishments are surveyed, many nonfarm workers—sole proprietors, unpaid volunteers, farm employees, private household employees, and unincorporated self-employed workers—are not covered. Also, people who work at more than one job are counted separately for each job held, which marginally inflates the numbers. Finally, the survey may also include "at least some undocumented immigrants" because the survey does not identify the legal status of the workers.[2]

The *total nonfarm payroll employment* series only counts individuals who show up on establishment payrolls, not workers defined as being employed in the companion "Household Data" *Current Population Survey* (CPS). The CPS is a different survey used to compute the monthly unemployment rate and defines a person as being employed if they are working, or if they have worked without pay for at least 15 hours in a family business, or if they had worked for one hour for pay or for profit during the previous survey week.

Coverage, Releases, and Revisions

The CES survey is conducted during the workweek containing the 12th of the month and includes approximately one-third of all nonfarm payrolls, representing approximately 80 percent of the workers who contribute to the GDP. The survey results are then released on the 7th of every subsequent month along with the CPS survey that is used to compute the unemployment rate.

Both surveys are then revised twice more in the succeeding two months to include additional survey information not available when the series were first released. Finally, annual benchmarks are conducted to further update the employment numbers.

The Historical Record

Figure 5-1 shows that total nonfarm employment turns down near or at the beginning of a recession. Total employment then starts to recover at, or shortly after, a recession ends. The figure also shows that total employment is slow to recover after a recession, often taking years to recover its pre-recession high.

---

[2] *The Employment Situation*, BLS News Release, March 2017.

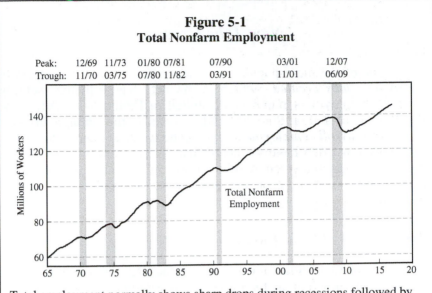

Figure 5-1
Total Nonfarm Employment

Peak:	12/69	11/73	01/80 07/81	07/90		03/01	12/07	
Trough:	11/70	03/75	07/80 11/82	03/91		11/01	06/09	

Total employment normally shows sharp drops during recessions followed by slow recoveries. Total employment declined by 6.3 percent during the Great Recession, and then took 75 months, or 6+ years, to recover its previous high.

    The total employment decline during the Great Recession was especially dramatic when approximately 8.7 million jobs were lost. To put this in perspective, this is about equal to the *entire* population of the state of New Jersey. The bottom line is that job losses can occur quickly when the economy is hit with a recession, and that the total employment numbers are painfully slow to come back.

Total Nonfarm Employment

Compiled by:	Bureau of Labor Statistics
Frequency:	Monthly
Release date:	First Friday of the following month
Revisions:	Preliminary estimate revised the next two months; regular benchmark revisions every year
Published data:	*Economic Indicators,* Council of Economic Advisors
	The Employment Situation, Bureau of Labor Statistics
Internet:	http://www.bls.gov
	http://www.EconSources.com

New Jobs Created

One of the more popular statistics in recent years is frequently called *new jobs created*—which is the net change in the monthly nonfarm employment numbers illustrated in Figure 5-1. Officially, the Bureau of Labor Statistics (BLS) calls it the *change in total nonfarm payroll employment* but nobody else seems to. For example, how often have we heard that "X thousand new jobs were created (or lost) in a given month," or how many times have we heard a politician say that he or she will create "X million new jobs if elected?"

The Monthly "New Jobs Created" Number

On the first Friday of every month the BLS reports on the latest employment situation in its *Employment Situation Summary*. This report, part of which is reproduced in Figure 5-3 on page 82, is the source of the new jobs created/lost number.[3] For example, the March 2017 report had 145,760,000 total non-farm jobs in February and 145,858,000 jobs in March, for a net change of 98,000 jobs.[4]

Monthly BLS Employment Numbers

Total nonfarm employment, more commonly called "total employment," comes from the *Current Employment Statistics (CES)* report that is compiled from monthly surveys of approximately 147,000 business establishments and government agencies that represent approximately 634,000 workers.

Because the establishment survey only counts the number of paid employment positions, the rise in the number of part-time jobs may overstate the employment situation. After all, if someone loses a

---

[3] Figure 5-3 appears on page 82 because we wanted to compare the monthly CES establishment survey with the monthly CPS household survey.

[4] This may seem like a lot for any one month, but it was widely panned in the press as being too little. *USA Today* described the report as being "feeble" and blamed the poor showing on "the weather, a late Easter that could have pushed the holiday hiring to April from March and a tight labor market." *Big Jobs Miss—Employers Add Disappointing 98,000 Positions in March*, April 8, 2017.

high paying full-time job and replaces it with three low-paying part-time ones, the new jobs created series would go up by two jobs. Because of this, monthly CES total employment usually grows faster than the number of people found to be employed in the monthly *Current Population Survey* (CPS) that covers households.

However, because the CES misses workers not on monthly establishment payrolls—sole proprietors, farm employees, private household employees, and unincorporated self-employed workers—changes in monthly employment totals may be understated.

The Historical Record

Figure 5-2 shows the monthly data from 1965 until the present. This series is somewhat volatile, which may in part be due to the fact that the monthly changes are the differences between two preliminary figures. Even so, the monthly *new jobs created* series appears to have value as a leading economic indicator for both recessions and subsequent recoveries.

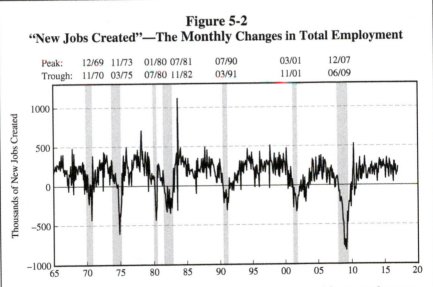

Figure 5-2
"New Jobs Created"—The Monthly Changes in Total Employment

| Peak: | 12/69 | 11/73 | 01/80 | 07/81 | 07/90 | 03/01 | 12/07 |
| Trough: | 11/70 | 03/75 | 07/80 | 11/82 | 03/91 | 11/01 | 06/09 |

The new job created series is the monthly change in total nonfarm employment. It is widely reported in the press and despite it volatility, it has characteristics of a leading economic indicator for recessions and economic expansions.

This pattern is easy to understand. After all, if labor markets get tight during the latter part of an expansion, business establishments may find it more difficult to find new employees and therefore add new jobs—hence smaller monthly new jobs created numbers are recorded just before a recession begins. And, as the recession is about to end, the number of new jobs created starts to grow again, foretelling of the subsequent recovery.

Why the Popularity?

Several reasons probably sum up the popularity of the series.

First, the title is catchy and is easy for the popular press to write about tens of thousands of jobs coming or going away. Second, the monthly number is easily found in the monthly *Employment Situation Summary*, even if it is based on preliminary data that have not been smoothed. Third, the number seems to have a life of its own in political circles where politicians seem to think that their personal philosophies and promised actions will actually add more jobs to the American economy than will the actions of other candidates.

Finally, the monthly numbers appear to be increasingly useful as a leading economic indicator for recessions despite their variability. All in all, if the numbers are big or perhaps small enough, or if they consistently go in one direction or the other, they can provide useful information about the economy's health, or lack thereof.

New Jobs Created	
Indicator status:	Leading for recessions; leading for recoveries
Compiled by:	Bureau of Labor Statistics
Frequency:	Monthly
Release date:	First Friday of the following month
Revisions:	Preliminary estimate revised the next two months; regular benchmark revisions every year
Published data:	*Economic Indicators,* Council of Economic Advisors
	The Employment Situation, Bureau of Labor Statistics
Internet:	http://www.bls.gov
	http://www.EconSources.com

Unemployment Rate

Unemployment numbers, specifically those in the *civilian unemployment rate*, or simply the *unemployment rate*, are among the most widely watched of all economic statistics. The rate can move as much as one or two percentage points in a short time, but it has remained within a much smaller range since the Great Depression of the 1930s when it peaked at nearly 25 percent.

How Are the Data Collected?

Unemployment data are collected monthly by the Census Bureau for the Bureau of Labor Statistics (BLS) using a survey covering about 60,000 households in approximately 2000 counties and independent cities, with coverage in all 50 states and the District of Columbia. The survey is called the Current Population Survey (CPS), and it is the source of most labor market data, including earnings differentials among worker groups, labor force participation rates, and demographic characteristics of workers.

For consistency, the CPS is conducted in the week containing the 19th day of the month, with most questions relating to the week of the 12th day of the month. The BLS then compiles the data and issues labor force information on the first Friday of the following month in the form of tables similar to those in Figure 5-3.[5] Because the unemployment rate appears along with the numbers for total employment and new jobs created, the BLS report is perhaps the U.S. Department of Commerce's most anticipated monthly release.

---

[5] From 1967 to 1993, the CPS questionnaire remained largely unchanged. During that time, however, a number of changes in the economy such as the growth of service jobs, the decline of factory jobs, the growing role of women, and the proliferation of alternative work schedules, took place. As a result, a computer-automated questionnaire with slightly revised questions was introduced in 1994 in an effort to achieve more accurate results. Under the old format, interviewers were equipped with a written list of questions, and the next question selected would be based on the answer to the previous question. Under the revised format, Census Bureau interviewers use portable computers that automatically select the next question for them. The revised questions and the automated system generate more reliable results, but they also resulted in unemployment numbers that were about one-half a percentage higher than before. Consequently, the numbers obtained today are not directly comparable to the ones obtained prior to 1994.

Figure 5-3
Major Indicators of Labor Market Activity*

HOUSEHOLD DATA

Table A-1. Employment status of the civilian population by sex and age (seasonally adjusted, numbers in thousands)

Employment status, sex, and age	Jan. 2017	Feb. 2017	Mar. 2017
TOTAL			
Civilian noninstitutional population	254,082	254,246	254,414
Civilian labor force	159,716	160,056	160,201
Employed	152,081	152,528	153,000
Unemployed	7,635	7,528	7,202
Unemployment rate	4.8	4.7	**4.5**
Not in labor force	94,366	94,190	94,213
Persons who currently want a job	5,739	5,597	5,781

ESTABLISHMENT DATA

Table B-1. Employees on nonfarm payrolls by industry sector and selected industry detail [seasonally adjusted, numbers in thousands]

Industry	Feb. 2017(p)	Mar. 2017(p)	Change from: Feb.2017 – Mar.2017
Total nonfarm	145,760	145,858	**98.0**
Total private	123,451	123,540	89.0
Goods-producing	19,941	19,969	28.0
Private service-producing	103,510	103,571	61.0
Government	22,309	22,318	9.0
Federal	2,817	2,816	1.0
State Government	5,085	5,086	1.0
Local Government	14,407	14,416	9.0

Source: The Employment Situation – March 2017.

*The monthly *Employment Situation* news release from the Bureau of Labor Statistics reports the results for the Current Population Survey (CPS) and the Current Employment Statistics (CES) programs at the same time. The CPS, also known as the Household Survey, appears in the top of the figure above. The CES, also known the Establishment Survey, appears in the lower part of the figure. Each survey has an extensive number of tables with data that provide an enormous amount of information on labor market activity. However, the two surveys use different definitions, methodologies, and sample sizes so the total number of employed persons reported in the two surveys will not match.

The Civilian Labor Force

One of the key measures that comes out of the CPS is the *civilian labor force,* which consists of all civilians 16 years or older who are not confined to an institution and are not on active duty in the armed forces. Since members of the armed forces are always considered to be employed, and since they could potentially make up a small—under two percent—but significant part of the labor force, the unemployment rate would be distorted if they were to be included.

The part of the definition concerning the noninstitutional population is also intended to exclude those confined to a mental institution, hospital, or prison. After all, they can hardly be expected to go out and seek, let alone hold, a job. Finally, the age limitation means that an enterprising 15-year-old working 50 hours a week cannot be counted as being either employed or unemployed—as the person is simply defined as not being in the labor force.

What Does It Take To Be Employed or Unemployed?

First, both employed and unemployed individuals must be part of the civilian labor force. Then, to be *employed,* an individual (a) had to have worked for as little as one hour for pay or for profit during the reference week, or (b) had to have worked for at least 15 hours for no pay in a family business during that period, or (c) had to have been temporarily absent from a job or business, whether or not they were being paid or were even looking for another job.

To be classified as *unemployed,* a person would have to be in the civilian labor force and jobless during the reference week. In addition, the person would have to be both available and looking for work— which means that the person had to have made at least one specific effort to find a job during the month preceding the survey week. Finally, someone who has been laid off but is waiting to be recalled would be unemployed even if they were not looking for other employment.

How Do We Get the Unemployment Rate?

This is the easy part. After we determine the number of unemployed persons, we divide them by the size of the civilian labor force. The March 2017 numbers looked like this:

$$\text{Unemployment rate} = \frac{\text{Number unemployed}}{\text{Civilian labor force}} = \frac{7,202,000}{160,201,000} = 4.5\%$$

Since the monthly survey data also identify the unemployed by sex, race, education, age, and marital status, we could also get the unemployment rate for adult men, adult women, teenagers, whites, blacks, and Hispanics. Unemployment rates for these groups are normally reported along with the overall civilian unemployment rate.

What about the Historical Record?

One of the striking things about the unemployment rate is the way it varies with the state of the economy. For example, whenever the economy is in a period of expansion as represented by the unshaded areas in Figure 5-4, the unemployment rate tends to fall— and relatively slowly at that.

However, when the economy is about to enter a recession, represented by the shaded areas in the figure, the unemployment rate moves up rapidly. Indeed, one of the major concerns of economists is the speed at which the unemployment rate can climb. For example, in

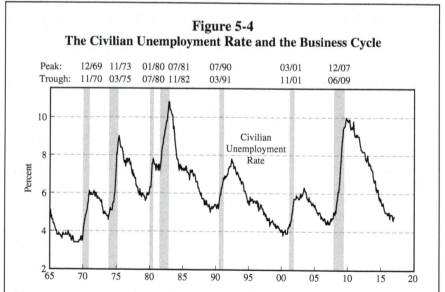

Figure 5-4
The Civilian Unemployment Rate and the Business Cycle

| Peak: | 12/69 | 11/73 | 01/80 | 07/81 | 07/90 | 03/01 | 12/07 |
| Trough: | 11/70 | 03/75 | 07/80 | 11/82 | 03/91 | 11/01 | 06/09 |

The unemployment rate acts like a leading indicator by turning up before a recession gets underway. Unfortunately, unemployment also tends to increase rapidly once a recession begins. After the recession is over, it then takes several years for the rate to get back down to its former pre-recession level.

May 2007 the unemployment rate was at 4.4 percent. Then, the Great Recession drove the rate to 10.0 percent in about two years. After that it took 10 full years for the rate to get back to its 4.4 percent pre-recession low.

Are Unemployment Numbers Really All That Significant?

More than you might think! Even a relatively small change in the monthly unemployment rate involves a large number of people. For example, with a civilian labor force of 160,201,000, an increase in the unemployment rate of just one-tenth of 1 percent would mean that an additional 160,201 individuals would be out of work! This is more than the total number of people currently living in Alexandria VA, Kansas City KS, Springfield MA, or Sunnyvale CA.

Incidentally, we might point out that the unemployment rate in the United States is measured differently than in many other nations. In the United States, we make an effort to look for the unemployed. In many other countries, people are not even counted as being unemployed until they actually show up to collect an unemployment check—which results in the unemployment rate being understated in those nations.

Have We Accounted for Everyone?

Not quite. Some individuals are *marginally attached workers.* These people want to work, are available for work, but have stopped looking for jobs sometime during the past 12 months. Had they bothered to look for work during the month prior to the survey week they would have been classified as unemployed, but their effort to find a job was not recent enough and so they are classified as "marginally" attached to the labor force.

A subset of the marginally attached workers category is *discouraged workers.* These individuals also want to work, are also available to work, and they have even looked for work sometime in the past 12 months, but they are not currently looking for work because they don't think that there are any jobs for which they would qualify. The main difference between the two groups is that the discouraged worker has simply given up while the marginally attached worker hasn't given up yet, but just hasn't looked recently.

Admittedly this is a pretty modest distinction to make between the two groups because it all hinges on whether or not one believes that it would be futile to look for a new job. Nevertheless, these two groups are neither employed nor unemployed—instead, they are simply not part of the labor force. In reality, marginally attached and discouraged workers are fairly common especially during periods of recession or in areas where homelessness is high.

The Unemployment Rate in Perspective

Aside from the pain, suffering, and sheer waste of resources implicit in the index, the unemployment rate has considerable value as an indicator of future economic activity. Although the warning period is relatively short, the series tends to be a reliable leading indicator of future economic downturns and a lagging indicator of impending recoveries.

Because it affects so many people, and because the unemployment rate is so difficult to bring down once it has risen sharply, it is also one of the most closely watched series in the economy.

Civilian Unemployment Rate	
Indicator status:	Leading for recessions; lagging for recoveries
Compiled by:	Bureau of Labor Statistics
Frequency:	Monthly
Release date:	Normally the first Friday of the following month
Revisions:	Monthly numbers not revised; annual revisions every January for the past 5 years to account for seasonal factors
Published data:	*Economic Indicators,* Council of Economic Advisors *The Employment Situation*, Bureau of Labor Statistics
Internet:	http://www.bls.gov http://www.EconSources.com

Help-Wanted Advertising

Economic statistics, like the economy itself, are sometimes in a state of transition. In fact, one of the more useful statistics that was designed to track job market conditions, The Conference Board's *Help-Wanted Advertising in Newspapers,* has been discontinued and replaced by *The Conference Board Help Wanted OnLine (HWOL)* series.[6] Both series appear in Figure 5-5 and both series appear to have done a reasonably good job predicting recessions by turning down well in advance of a general economic downturn.

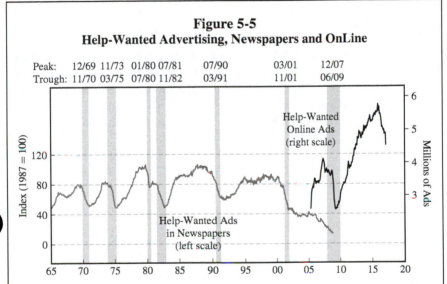

Figure 5-5
Help-Wanted Advertising, Newspapers and OnLine

| Peak: | 12/69 | 11/73 | 01/80 | 07/81 | 07/90 | 03/01 | 12/07 |
| Trough: | 11/70 | 03/75 | 07/80 | 11/82 | 03/91 | 11/01 | 06/09 |

The Help-Wanted Advertising Index was based on the number of classified ads in 51 selected cities. Historically, the index has been a fairly reliable leading indicator of impending economic downturns. The Conference Board's new online index, the HWOL, likewise shows promise as a leading indicator.

---

[6] The monthly newspaper index was compiled by The Conference Board and was available from 1951 to July 2008 with 1987 used as the base year.

The Evolution of Help-Wanted Ads

Help-wanted ads have long been of interest to economists. Some of the earliest series were compiled by the National Bureau of Economic Research (NBER) which had a *Help-Wanted Advertising in Newspapers for United States* series that went from 1919 to 1960, and was followed by a revised series that went from 1951 to 1966.[7] The series was later transferred to The Conference Board and was the predominant one until it was replaced by the current HWOL series.

As for The Conference Board's newspaper index, data on the number of help-wanted classified ads printed in 51 cities around the country was collected. In each city, a count of all classified ads was taken from a single newspaper, and the total was adjusted for both seasonal patterns and the number of days in each calendar month. The count for each city was then weighted according to the size of the labor market in the region and, after some other minor adjustments, compiled and released.[8]

But, by the early 2000s, as can be seen in Figure 5-5, something was happening that caused a significant change in the reliability of the newspaper index. The Internet, of course, along with changes in people's job search behavior, were thought to be the reasons. After all, when someone wanted a job they could search a company's website, or they simply searched for a job on one of the many job search sites that were available on the web. Some people still consulted the local paper for employment opportunities, but in general the Internet changed people's job search habits.

In response to these behavioral and structural changes, The Conference Board decided to develop a similar series, only this time it would focus exclusively on help-wanted ads that appeared online rather than in newspapers. Thus the new series—the HWOL—was born. This new measure counts the number of new jobs and jobs reposted from the previous month that appear on more than 16,000 job sources including traditional job boards, corporate job boards and social media sites. Finally, job openings are compiled in such a way as to eliminate duplication.[9]

---

[7] The *FRED Economic Data* database at the Federal Reserve Bank of St. Louis is a good source for these early NBER series.

[8] See The Help-Wanted Index: Technical Description and Behavioral Trends, Conference Board Report No. 716.

[9] Little else is known about the current methodology used to compile the HWOL series as it is proprietary. The data is currently collected by Haver Analytics, a provider of time series data for the global and research community. A different vendor collected the data for the earlier years of the series.

Help-Wanted Ads as Economic Indicators

Because the new HWOL series started in May 2005, the series has too short a history to fairly evaluate it as a reliable economic indicator. Even so it appears to be a capable replacement for the newspapers series. With the exception of the newspaper series performance in the early 2000s, both indices tended to peak several months before a recession set in, and the amount of lead time was fairly consistent.

Both series also tended to fall throughout the recessions and, with the exception of the newspapers series in 2001, then bottomed out just as, or shortly after, the recession ended making them coincident indicators for the end of the recession.

Finally, the data were not subject to revision, so we did not have to wait for additional data to see how a particular month fared.

In Summary

Help-wanted ads, whether they appeared in newspapers or currently appear online, have had a long and distinguished history of being reliable economic indicators. Such indicators are indeed rare which makes them important to those who monitor business cycles.

Help-Wanted OnLine Advertising	
Indicator status:	Leading indicator for recession; coincident for recoveries
Compiled by:	The Conference Board, 845 Third Avenue, New York, NY 10022
Frequency:	Monthly
Release date:	Normally the 1st Monday after close of the reference month
Revisions:	Methodology not disclosed
Published data:	Monthly Conference Board press releases
Internet:	http://www.conference-board.org/ http://www.EconSources.com

New Jobless Claims

The Employment and Training Administration (ETA) in the U.S. Department of Labor has a useful economic indicator called *unemployment insurance weekly claims*—although it is more commonly called "new jobless claims" or "initial unemployment claims." The data cover new unemployment insurance claims that are generated at the state level and are then published as part of a combined federal/state program.[10]

The data are published weekly in both seasonally adjusted and unadjusted formats. Because the initial weekly numbers are subject to such wide variations, the data are smoothed with a four-week moving average. The smoothed data series is shown in Figure 5-6.

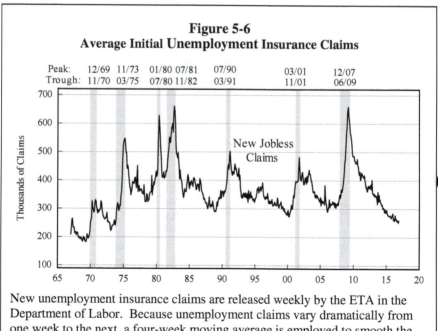

Figure 5-6
Average Initial Unemployment Insurance Claims

New unemployment insurance claims are released weekly by the ETA in the Department of Labor. Because unemployment claims vary dramatically from one week to the next, a four-week moving average is employed to smooth the data.

---

[10] U.S. Employment and Training Administration, *Unemployment Insurance Weekly Claims*

Why New Jobless Claims Are an Economic Indicator

Because labor is usually considered to be a variable cost, meaning that the number of workers employed varies with changes in the level of production, new claims for unemployment insurance are intuitively appealing as an economic indicator.

Indeed, Figure 5-6 shows that new claims tend to decline during expansionary periods and then rise sharply several months before a recession actually begins. This behavior makes the series a *leading* indicator when it comes to forecasting peaks in economic activity. The series also tends to decline at about the time the recession ends, which makes it a *coincident* indicator for recoveries. Because of the relatively uniform lead times for the turning points, The Conference Board includes the series as one of the ten components for its *Leading Economic Index (LEI)*.

The four-week moving average is the important part of the statistic, however, not just the weekly initial claims numbers that are generally reported by the press. Because initial weekly claims data tend to vary so widely from one period to the next, it is important to focus on the underlying trend to get a better measure of labor market conditions.[11]

New Jobless Claims	
Indicator status:	Leading for recessions; coincident for recoveries
Compiled by:	Employment & Training Administration, Dept. of Labor
Frequency:	Weekly
Release date:	Advance figure, week after close of the last reporting week
Revisions:	Previous two weeks revised with each weekly release; annual revisions in January for several years back
Published data:	*Economic Indicators*, Council of Economic Advisors *Unemployment Insurance Weekly* Claims Report, Employment and Training Administration,
Internet:	http://www.dol.gov/ui/data.pdf http://www.EconSources.com

---

[11] Some states tie people's jobless payments to earnings in a base period such as the previous quarter. This often causes people to delay unemployment filings until a more favorable base period can be reported.

Chapter 6

SPENDING, PROFITS, and EXPECTATIONS

Consumer Spending

Spending by consumers is a key measure of the economy's health. It is tracked monthly by the Bureau of Economic Analysis (BEA) in the U.S. Department of Commerce and is reported in both current and constant (inflation adjusted) dollars. The monthly series, more formally known as *personal consumption expenditures* or PCE for short, is used to produce the quarterly consumer spending component of GDP.

The category of monthly personal consumption expenditures illustrated in Table 6-1 is easily the single largest component of GDP, accounting for almost 70 percent of all spending in the National Income and Product Accounts. The fact that it is such a large portion of GDP requires that we take a close look at it, especially to see if it tends to change over time.

How Does Consumer Spending Behave?

It turns out that the category of personal consumption expenditures is the most stable component of spending in the economy.[1] The current dollar series, the one not adjusted for inflation, is

---

[1] The reader may want to refer to Table 4-1 on page 59 to see how the covariance of changes in real personal consumption expenditure compares to other major GDP components. Additionally, note that the quarterly changes of PCE subcomponents— durable goods, nondurable goods, and services—are more stable than all other spending categories with the exception of state and local government spending.

Table 6-1
Personal Consumption Expenditures, Billions of Dollars

	Current	Constant (2009$)	% GDP
Gross domestic product	*$19,007.3*	*$16,842.4*	*100.0*
Personal consumption expenditures	*13,096.4*	*11,679.5*	*68.9*
Durable goods	1,435.0	1,133.9	7.5
Motor vehicles and parts	478.6	437.6	2.5
Furnishings and household equipment	321.5	34.9	1.7
Recreational goods and vehicles	413.7	635.0	2.2
Other durable goods	221.2	217.6	1.2
Nondurable goods	2,781.2	2,532.2	14.6
Food and beverages	939.8	859.2	4.9
Clothing and footwear	382.0	364.1	2.0
Gasoline and other energy goods	305.5	282.7	1.6
Other nondurable goods	1,153.9	1,035.4	5.6
Services	8,880.2	7,561.2	46.7
Housing and utilities	2,372.3	2,015.2	12.5
Health care	2,261.1	2,019.0	11.9
Transportation services	390.6	344.3	2.1
Recreation services	504.6	434.7	2.7
Food service and a combination	870.9	728.5	4.6
Financial services and insurance	986.4	730.9	5.2
Other services	1,494.0	652.4	3.9
Gross private domestic investment	*3,146.5*	*2,898.4*	*16.6*
Net exports of goods and services	*(558.4)*	*(602.7)*	*(2.9)*
Government consumption and gross invest.	3,322.7	*2,895.2*	*17.5*

Source: BEA, first quarter advance 2017 estimates

shown in Figure 6-1 along with a shorter series expressed in real or constant 2009 dollars. The stability of the current dollar series is such that it usually goes up, regardless of whether the economy is expanding or not. To illustrate, the current dollar series decreased only 73 times out of the 625 months shown in the figure.

We get a better view of monthly consumer spending when the series is adjusted for inflation by using constant 2009 dollars. The shorter constant dollar series, only available since 1999, turned down 114 times out of the 216 months in Figure 6-1—with 10 of those decreases occurring during the 18 months of the Great Recession.

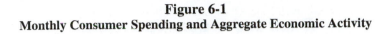

Figure 6-1

Monthly Consumer Spending and Aggregate Economic Activity

Peak:	12/69	11/73	01/80	07/81	07/90	03/01	12/07
Trough:	11/70	03/75	07/80	11/82	03/91	11/01	06/09

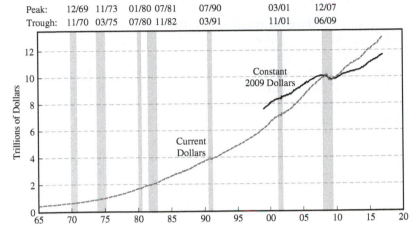

Personal consumer spending in current dollars is among the most predictable of all economic statistics because it usually just goes up, primarily because of inflation. When the distortions of inflation are removed, the monthly constant dollar series (only available starting 1999) is a better measure of how well we are doing, rather than of where we are headed.

The majority of current and constant dollar downturns were collectively smaller than their increases; otherwise neither series would have been able to increase over time. In addition, neither series can be used to predict when changes in future economic activity are about to happen because they themselves are the major part of economic activity. Because of this, PCE expenditures are simply indicators of how well we are doing.

Personal Consumption Expenditures

Indicator status:	None
Compiled by:	Bureau of Economic Analysis
Frequency:	Monthly
Release date:	End of month following releases and updates of GDP
Revisions:	Revisions of estimates to beginning of previous quarter
Published data:	*Survey of Current Business*, U.S. Department of Commerce
Internet:	http://www.bea.gov
	http://www.EconSources.com

Retail and E-Commerce Sales

To collect data on retail sales, the Census Bureau conducts a monthly retail trade survey that covers approximately 4700 retail and food service firms. The first estimate of retail sales is called *advance monthly sales for retail trade and food services* and appears about two weeks after the close of the reference month. Retail sales are those made from retail trade establishments that are engaged in selling merchandise in small quantities to the general public.[2]

The advance series is revised two more times before the numbers become final, but advance sales get the attention because they come out first. Breakdowns are available for a variety of industries, including building materials, automotive dealers, grocery stores, eating and drinking establishments, and many others.[3]

The Historical Record

Figure 6-2 shows the historical series of advance monthly retail sales from the *Advance Monthly Sales for Retail and Food Services*.[4] The advance release is not adjusted for inflation, although constant dollar data are available shortly thereafter.

The data reflect discretionary expenditures of the consumer sector, as well as some spending at retail locations by governmental and business units. However, because the newer retail sales series in the figure only spans two recessions, we can only speculate as to how

---

[2] The two principal types of establishments are "Store retailers [that] operate fixed point of sale locations, located and designed to attract a high volume of walk-in customers (and) non-store retailers [that] serve the general public, but . . . include paper electronic catalogs, door-to-door solicitations, in-home demonstrations, 'infomercials,' selling from portable stalls or through vending machines." *Monthly & Annual Retail Trade FAQ* website, U.S. Department of Commerce.

[3] The retail sales series is different from most NIPA data in that the monthly sales figures are not annualized. Instead, monthly numbers report on sales for the period and annual sales are determined by adding up the sales for each of the individual months. The series is, however, adjusted for seasonal, holiday, and trading day differences.

[4] The *Advance Monthly Retail Trade Report* is available in a PDF format. The *Monthly Retail Trade Report* is only available in the form of Excel and ASCII tables.

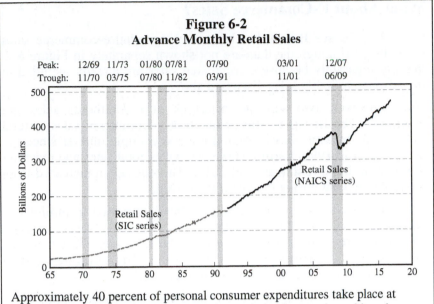

Figure 6-2
Advance Monthly Retail Sales

Peak:	12/69	11/73	01/80 07/81	07/90		03/01	12/07
Trough:	11/70	03/75	07/80 11/82	03/91		11/01	06/09

Approximately 40 percent of personal consumer expenditures take place at retail stores. Retail sales are strong during periods of expansion, although some volatility is due to big-ticket items such as automobiles and furniture.

it will perform during the next one.[5] Even so it seems reasonable to assume that consumers will be reluctant to reduce spending until they are forced to, which explains why the series did not decline until it was well into the Great Recession. This pattern would make it a lagging indicator for recessions if it were to repeat. Advance monthly retail sales also turned down during three of the last four months of the 2001 recession, making it consistent with the lagging indicator observation.

The good news is that retail sales picked up before the economy recovered from the Great Recession, making it a possible leading indicator for recoveries. Advance sales also increased during the latter part of the 2001 recession, so perhaps the pattern will continue.

---

[5] The two series in Figure 6-2 are the result of the Commerce Department's switch from the older Standard Industrial Classification (SIC) to the newer North American Industrial Classification System (NAICS). The switch affected the number of firms in the survey, and hence the volume of sales covered.

What About E-Commerce Sales?

The Census Bureau has been tracking retail e-commerce sales since 1999, although the data are not shown separately in Figure 6-2. We say separately because e-commerce sales are already included in the advance monthly sales discussed above.

However, two separate measures of e-commerce sales are available. The first is a ratio of quarterly e-commerce sales to total sales. This measure has increased for every single quarter since the series began in 1999, starting at 0.6 percent of total sales and reaching 8.5 percent in the first quarter of 2017. The sales even increased from 3.6 to 4.0 percent during the Great Recession.

The second e-commerce sales series is reported in millions of current dollars and, like the first series, almost always went up although there were three exceptions. The first was when it turned down in the latter part of the 2001 recession. The series then turned down twice in the middle of the Great Recession.

About all we can conclude from e-commerce sales at this point is that they are a small but steadily growing component of total advance retail sales. They certainly indicate a significant ongoing structural change in the economy, and one worth watching as well, but neither quarterly e-commerce series tells us much else about the economy.

Retail and E-Commerce Sales	
Indicator status:	Lagging for recessions; leading for recoveries
Compiled by:	U.S. Census Bureau
Frequency:	Monthly for the *Advance Monthly Retail Sales*
	Quarterly for the *Quarterly E-Commerce Report*
Release date:	Approximately two weeks after the close of the month
	for *Advance* Retail *Sales*; about six weeks after
	the *Quarterly E-Commerce Report*
Revisions:	Advance, preliminary and revised in subsequent months
Published data:	*Economic Indicators*, Council of Economic Advisors
	Advance Monthly Retail Sales, U.S. Dept. of Commerce
Internet:	https://www.census.gov/retail/index.html
	http://www.EconSources.com

Wholesale Sales

The series of monthly sales by merchant wholesalers, officially known as *monthly wholesale trade*, provides yet another view of how aggregate economic activity is performing. However, the story is not always clear because the turning points in the series gave us inconsistent warnings of changes in future economic conditions.

Conducting the Survey

The monthly wholesale sales series is derived from the *Monthly Wholesale Trade Survey* (MWTS) conducted by the U.S. Census Bureau.[6]   The mail-out/mail-back survey covers approximately 4200 firms that are primarily engaged in wholesale trade—jobbers, industrial distributors, exporters, importers, and others who sell goods on their own account. Manufacturing firms that sell directly to the retailer, merchandise or commodity brokers, and merchants that work on commission are excluded.

The most recent monthly figures are always "preliminary" and are released approximately 40 days after the close of the data month. The preliminary figures are then revised again in each of the two subsequent months. The data, shown in Figure 6-3, are adjusted for seasonal and trading-day differences, but not for inflation.

Why the Interest in Wholesale Sales?

First, the series reports on an important segment of the economy. Second, it may also be due to the assumption that whatever happens to wholesalers will also happen to retailers and finally to consumers. As for being an economic indicator, peaks in the wholesale series sometimes lead, and sometimes lag, the beginning of a recession. When it comes to the ensuing recovery, the troughs in the wholesale series are sometimes coincident with, and at other times lead, the economic expansion.

---

[6] The series is reported in the *Monthly Wholesale Trade: Sales and Inventories* news release, Census Bureau, U.S. Department of Commerce.

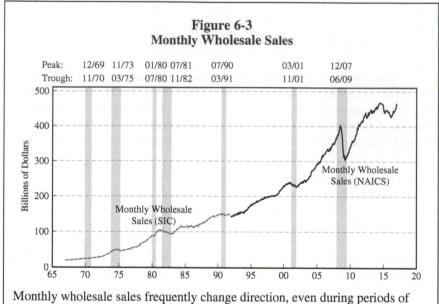

Figure 6-3
Monthly Wholesale Sales

Peak:	12/69	11/73	01/80 07/81	07/90		03/01	12/07
Trough:	11/70	03/75	07/80 11/82	03/91		11/01	06/09

Monthly wholesale sales frequently change direction, even during periods of sustained economic growth. However, the sharp downturn during the Great Recession indicates that the series is becoming more volatile than in the past.

Data on wholesale trade are used by the Bureau of Economic Analysis to prepare quarterly GDP estimates, but the monthly wholesale trade series has no value as a predictor of future business cycle turning points. Instead, the series generally tends to go up when the economy is expanding and then down when the economy is contracting—so it performs fairly well as a coincident economic indicator that tells us how the economy is currently doing.

Monthly Wholesale Trade	
Indicator status:	Coincident economic indicator
Compiled by:	U.S. Census Bureau
Frequency:	Monthly
Release date:	About 40 days after the close of the data month
Revisions:	Preliminary estimates revised twice monthly; annual revisions with benchmark revisions every few years
Published data:	*Monthly Wholesale Trade*, Census Bureau
	Economic Indicators, Council of Economic Advisors
Internet:	http://www.census.gov/wholesale/index.html
	http://www.EconSources.com

Consumer Expectations and Confidence

Because the consumer sector makes up such a large portion of the overall economy, it is reasonable to assume that people's decisions to spend or save can be affected by the confidence and expectations they have in the economy or in their own financial situation. These considerations have been historically important, and two highly regarded series have been tracking these factors. The first deals with expectations; the second deals with confidence.

Consumer Expectations

The first of the two series is derived from a Consumer Sentiment survey compiled by the Institute for Social Research (ISR) at the University of Michigan. To do so, the ISR conducts a telephone survey of 500 randomly selected individuals from all states except Alaska and Hawaii. The sample is closed, which means that only individuals initially selected for the sample are contacted for the survey. However, because of a rotating design, a new group of consumers appears in the sample every month to assure continuity of results.[7]

One component of the Consumer Sentiment survey is the *Index of Consumer Expectations* shown in Figure 6-4. Historically the index performed so well as a leading indicator of future economic activity that it was included as one of the individual components in The Conference Board's *Leading Economic Index*. The expectations results are made available for release during the last week of the reporting month and are not revised.[8]

---

[7] According to Richard T. Curtin at the ISR, "The sample is designed to maximize the study of change by incorporating a rotating panel sample design in an ongoing monthly survey program. For each monthly sample, an independent cross-section sample of households is drawn. The respondents chosen in this drawing are then reinterviewed six months later. A rotating panel design results, and the total sample for any one survey is normally made up of 55 percent new respondents, and 45 percent being reviewed for the second time." *Surveys of Consumers*, Survey Research Center.

[8] The monthly reports are available on a subscription basis. For further information contact Surveys of Consumers, Survey Research Center, University of Michigan, 426 Thompson Street, Ann Arbor, MI, 48104-2321.

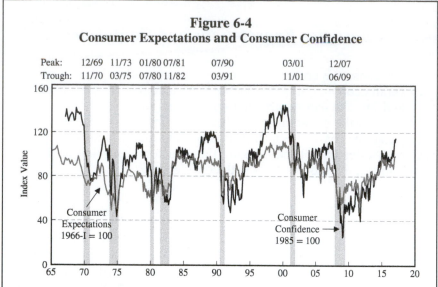

Figure 6-4
Consumer Expectations and Consumer Confidence

| Peak: | 12/69 | 11/73 | 01/80 07/81 | 07/90 | 03/01 | 12/07 |
| Trough: | 11/70 | 03/75 | 07/80 11/82 | 03/91 | 11/01 | 06/09 |

Consumer expectations peak a little earlier than consumer confidence, but both function well as leading economic indicators. However, ISR's expectations index is a component of The Conference Board's *Leading Economic Index.*

Consumer Confidence

In 1967, The Conference Board (TCB) introduced its own *Consumer Confidence Survey.*[9] This survey takes place during the first two weeks of every month and covers 5000 households. Consumer confidence is expressed as an index with a base of 1985 = 100, and it covers a number of categories, including appraisals of the current business situation; expectations of business conditions, employment, and income for the next six months; plans to buy automobiles, homes, and major appliances in the next six months; and, questions on vacation plans.

The Conference Board's index, like the ISR's expectations index, is available monthly and performs quite well as a leading indicator for recessions. Figure 6-4 shows that it tends to peak before the economy slides into recession, although it has an inconsistent

---

[9] See the *Consumer Confidence Survey,* a monthly report from the Consumer Research Center at The Conference Board, 845 Third Ave, New York, NY 10022. The Conference Board also compiles the *Leading Economic Index.*

record of predicting when a recession will end. As for timing, ISR's expectations report appears a month earlier than TCB's confidence report. This is because data from ISR's phone survey are collected and released in the same month, while data in TCB's Consumer Confidence Survey are collected with a mail survey that is not closed out until around the 18th of the month, with results compiled and posted in the following month.   To illustrate, TCB's Consumer Confidence Survey of March 28, 2017 reported the index value for February, while the March 31, 2017 ISR report covered March as well as February.

Summing Up

So what, you might ask, is the major distinction between consumer confidence and consumer expectations? Consumer *confidence* according to TCB, is an indicator "that measures the degree of optimism that consumers feel about the overall state of the economy and their personal financial situation" whereas consumer *sentiment* is an "economic indicator of the overall health of the economy as determined by consumer opinion."[10] The major difference, then, is that TCB deals with *optimism* while ISR deals with *opinion*. Got it?

That may not seem like much of a distinction, and perhaps that is why the two series behave about the same—but at least both tend to move in the same general direction whether they are going up or down.

Consumer Expectations and Confidence	
Indicator status:	Both series: leading for recessions, coincident or lagging otherwise
Compiled by:	*Consumer Confidence Survey,* The Conference Board
	Consumer Expectations, Institute for Social Research, University of Michigan
Frequency:	Monthly (both)
Release date:	Latter part of reference month (both)
Published data:	*Consumer Confidence Survey*, subscription from TCB
	Consumer Expectations, subscription basis from ISR
Internet:	www.conference-board.org/data/consumerconfidence.cfm
	http://www.sca.isr.umich.edu/
	http://www.EconSources.com

---

[10] From www.conference-board.org, April 22, 2017.

Employment Cost Index

The quarterly *employment cost index* (ECI) series is designed to measure the change in the cost of labor over time. The series includes wages, salaries, and the employer's cost of employee benefits at approximately 6800 private business and 1400 state and local government locations. The popular measure, expressed only as an index and not in dollar amounts, "measures the change in the cost of labor, free from the influence of employment shifts among occupations and industries."[11]

Like most other series, we can focus on the level of the index, or changes in the level. A popular version, shown in Figure 6-5, is in

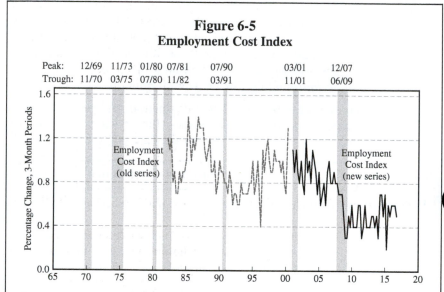

Figure 6-5
Employment Cost Index

| Peak: | 12/69 | 11/73 | 01/80 | 07/81 | 07/90 | 03/01 | 12/07 |
| Trough: | 11/70 | 03/75 | 07/80 | 11/82 | 03/91 | 11/01 | 06/09 |

The employment cost index is often used as an escalator for national defense contracts and numerous private and government pay scales. It is thought to be an indicator of future inflation and is closely watched by the Fed, but it has no properties as an indicator of future changes in aggregate economic activity.

---

[11] Technical Note, *Employment Cost Index—March 2017 News Release*, Bureau of Labor Statistics, U.S. Department of Labor. This news release has labor costs indexed to 2005=100 and percent changes for 3 months periods.

terms of percentage changes of quarterly data, although percentage changes over 12-month periods are also available.

Uses and Users of the ECI

Because the ECI reflects employment cost trends, and because the cost of labor is such a large component of total production costs, it is often used in escalator clauses. The federal government uses the series to adjust defense contracts, and it is even used to determine allowable increases in Medicare hospital charges.

The series has also been used in numerous private and public sector collective bargaining agreements. Federal pay adjustments for the U.S. Congress, federal judges, and senior government officials are also tied to the ECI, as are the salaries of many state officials.

Finally, the Federal Reserve System uses the ECI as an indicator of future inflation—as a tool to help predict where we are headed, rather than to tell us where we have been. In fact, the Fed seldom raises the discount rate without voicing some concern over increases in current or expected future labor costs.

What about the Cost of an Employee?

The quarterly ECI survey also provides data on the dollar cost of employees to their employers, but the data are published in a separate news release.[12] These data are reported in cost per hour worked and also as a percent of total compensation for occupational and industry groups. However, like the ECI, the dollar cost of employee compensation has no value as an indicator of future GDP changes.

Employment Cost Index	
Indicator status:	No status with regard to future economic activity
Compiled by:	Bureau of Labor Statistics
Frequency:	Quarterly
Release date:	End of the month following the reference quarter
Published data:	*Employment Cost Index,* Department of Labor
	Economic Indicators, Council of Economic Advisors
Internet:	http://www.bls.gov/news.release/pdf/eci.pdf

---

[12] See *Employer Costs for Employee Compensation,* Bureau of Labor Statistics.

Corporate Profits

Corporate profits are often in the news, especially when they are abnormally high or low, or when they come from a well-known company like Apple, IBM, General Motors, or Microsoft. But, of what value are they to those who are interested in the arrival of the next recession, or the beginning of the next recovery? Well, the Bureau of Economic Analysis in the Department of Commerce can help because it compiles a series called *corporate profits after tax*. These profits are reported for domestic financial and nonfinancial firms, including manufacturing, trade, transportation, and public utilities.

Collecting the Data

First, the Internal Revenue Service provides the Census Bureau with an annually list of firms with total net assets of $250,000 or more. The Census Bureau then associates NIACS codes to each for sampling and stratification purposes. Approximately 11,000 U.S. corporations are randomly selected from this list and are surveyed quarterly for estimated statements of income, retained earnings, balance sheet items, and even financial ratios.

These data are published in the Census Bureau's "Quarterly Financial Report" (QFR) which is the primary data source for the corporate profits after tax category that appears in the National Income and Product Accounts.[13] The QFR is released approximately 45 days after the close of the quarter, along with revisions to the two previous quarters.

Good, But Hard to Find

The leading indicator properties of corporate profits after tax are shown in Figure 6-6. In fact, with the exception of the 1973–75 recession, corporate profits have stalled or turned down well in advance of the decline in economic activity. If the series has a

---

[13] *Quarterly Financial Report: U.S. Manufacturing, Mining, Wholesale Trade, and Selected Service Industries,* U.S. Census Bureau, Department of Commerce. Also see *Updated Summary of NIPA Methodologies,* U.S. Census Bureau.

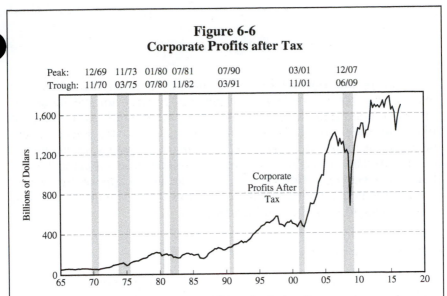

Figure 6-6
Corporate Profits after Tax

Peak:	12/69	11/73	01/80 07/81	07/90		03/01	12/07
Trough:	11/70	03/75	07/80 11/82	03/91		11/01	06/09

The most popular of the corporate profits series is the after-tax measure shown above. Because data are collected from quarterly corporate reports, the series is only available quarterly, and then after a considerable delay.

limitation, it is that it is reported on a delayed basis, and even then it is buried in the GDP accounts.

The fact that it is so hard to find may be the reason that people sometimes confuse the quarterly corporate profits reports we hear about in the press with the comprehensive series in Figure 6-6. The latter is worth watching; the former, less so.

Corporate Profits	
Indicator status:	Leading indicator for recessions; coincident for recoveries
Compiled by:	Census Bureau and the Bureau of Economic Analysis
Frequency:	Quarterly
Release date:	Approximately 45 days following the close of the quarter
Revisions:	A second, final, revision appears 45 days after the first, or 90 days after the end of the quarter
Published data:	*Economic Indicators,* Council of Economic Advisors *Survey of Current Business*, U.S. Department of Commerce
Internet:	http://www.bea.gov

Beige Book

There are any number of economic statistics that affect our daily lives. Most, like GDP, the unemployment rate, and industrial production, are statistics in the true sense of the word. Other reports, like *The Beige Book*, aren't really statistics at all, but they are nevertheless important. *The Beige Book*, a summary of economic conditions and collection of anecdotal information prepared by the Fed, is released eight times a year, and—because it appears two weeks prior to the Fed's monetary policy meetings—it is often treated as if it were a guide to what the Fed intends to do.

The Demise of Discretionary Fiscal Policy

Discretionary fiscal policy, our federal government's taxing and spending behavior, has become so politically driven and so cumbersome in its application that it cannot respond very effectively to rapid changes in economic conditions. We only need to recall the difficulties faced by the Obama administration when it tried to enact the $787 billion American Recovery and Reinvestment Act (ARRA) during the depths of the Great Recession to comprehend this.

After a difficult congressional battle, ARRA became law in February 2009 despite the fact that it only received 4 percent of House Republican votes and no votes from Senate Republicans. This extremely partisan vote is a stark reminder that fiscal policy is often driven by party affiliation, and not the state of the economy. As a result, we rely more on programs that are more or less fixed, such as progressive income tax rates, unemployment insurance compensation, welfare subsidies, and other such programs that economists call automatic stabilizers.

The Fed and Monetary Policy

The policymaking void left by the demise of discretionary fiscal policy has largely been filled by the Federal Reserve System's use of monetary policy. Conceptually, monetary policy is nothing more than increasing or decreasing the size of the money supply in order to affect the availability and cost of credit. The laws of supply and demand reign supreme here: if the Fed increases the money supply, interest rates go down; if the Fed reduces or tightens the money supply, interest rates go up.[14]

Monetary Policy Decision Variables

The policy makers at the Fed not only watch all of the statistics explored in this book, but they also want to know as much as possible about other economic conditions that are more difficult to quantify. Besides, the Fed has a long tradition of considering the regional perspectives of its twelve district banks before it makes its monetary policy decisions. As a result, by 1970 these regional viewpoints were formalized in a confidential—for policymakers only—report called *The Red Book*.[15]

By the early 1980s, however, Congress was pressing the Fed to be more open with respect to its monetary policy making. The result was the release of *The Red Book* to the public in 1983. To mark this change, the cover of the report was changed to beige, hence what is known today as *The Beige Book*.

The modern report is approximately 30–40 pages long and draws on a variety of information from the board of directors at the Fed's twelve district banks, branch bank directors, contacts in the business community, and so on. A summary of national economic conditions, shown in Figure 6-7, makes up the first part of *The Beige Book*. Summaries of economic conditions in each of the twelve districts make up the remainder, but there are no statistical tables.[16]

The summary describes conditions in the areas of consumer spending, real estate and construction, manufacturing, banking and finance, insurance, labor markets, and agriculture and natural resources. If that doesn't leave you bleary-eyed, you can pursue the full 36 pages of similar commentary at the regional level.[17]

---

[14] Assuming *ceteris paribus* of course, the assumption that all other things remain constant while the money supply changes.

[15] See David Fettig, Arthur J. Rolnick, and David E. Runkle, "The Federal Reserve's Beige Book, A Better Mirror than Crystal Ball," *The Region*, Federal Reserve Bank of Minneapolis, March 1999, for an excellent history and summary (the article can be retrieved from either of the two websites listed at the end of this section).

[16] The summary in Figure 6-7 also appeared in the 7th edition of this little *Guide*, but we decided to keep it because it was prepared in early 2009, five quarters after the Great Recession started. It seems to describe an economy in modest decline, but certainly not the description we would expect of an economy in the depths of its worst recession since the 1930s!

[17] We have never, in fact, met a single living economist outside the Fed who has read any of the *Beige Books* from beginning to end.

Figure 6-7
The Beige Book—Summary of Commentary of
Current Economic Conditions by Federal Reserve District

Reports from the Federal Reserve Banks indicate that overall economic activity contracted further or remained weak. However, five of the twelve Districts noted a moderation in the pace of decline, and several saw signs that activity in some sectors was stabilizing at a low level.

Manufacturing activity weakened across a broad range of industries in most Districts, with only a few exceptions. Nonfinancial service activity continued to contract across Districts. Retail spending remained sluggish, although some Districts noted a slight improvement in sales compared with the previous reporting period. Residential real estate markets continued to be weak. Home prices and construction were still falling in most areas, but better-than-expected buyer traffic led to a scattered pickup in sales in a number of Districts. Nonresidential real estate conditions continued to deteriorate. Difficulty obtaining commercial real estate financing was constraining construction and investment activity. Spending on business travel declined as corporations cut back. Reports on tourism were mixed. Bankers reported tight credit conditions, rising delinquencies, and some deterioration of loan quality.

Agricultural conditions were generally favorable across Districts, although drought conditions persisted in the Dallas and San Francisco Districts. The Districts reporting on energy said reduced demand, high inventories, and lower prices led to steep cutbacks in oil and natural gas drilling and production activity. The Minneapolis, Kansas City, and Dallas Districts noted declines in employment in the oil and gas extraction industry.

NOTE: The reader may find the above summary a bit rosy considering that it was prepared near the bottom of the 2008–09 Great Recession. The authors certainly do.

The above *Beige Book* summary was prepared by the Federal Reserve Bank of Dallas and was made public two weeks prior to the April 28–29 monetary policy meeting in 2009. The Fed cautions that the Beige Book comments are commentaries only and not the official views of the Fed.

Source: *Beige Book*, April 15, 2009

Mirror or Crystal Ball?

The question facing Fed watchers is the extent to which *The Beige Book* provides us with an insight into the Fed's likely intentions. Do statements such as "Most Districts continued to report weakness in labor markets and some downward pressure on wages, although benefit costs continued to increase" mean that the Fed will change interest rates?

Economists have tried to answer this question by assigning numerical scores to various aspects of more than 300 *Beige Books*. The scores were then analyzed to see if they could improve on the estimates given by the computerized forecasting models already used by the Fed. One study found that *The Beige Book* was of some help. Another, and more complete, study found that a close examination of *The Beige Book* could not improve on the quality of output already provided by private sector forecasts. According to the latter, "the media and Fed watchers would do well to put aside *The Beige Book* and focus on private sector forecasts in their attempts to predict monetary policy."[18]

So, why should a little volume devoted to understanding everyday economic statistics bother with *The Beige Book*? For one, any given report is quite detailed and generally covers important regional developments in labor markets, agricultural outlooks, industrial production, the retail trades, and so on: just the kinds of things that are not always well revealed by statistics. For another, we hear about it in the press often enough to realize that we should know more about it. Finally, it is nice to know some of what the Fed knows—even if the product might be more of a mirror than a crystal ball.

The Beige Book	
Indicator status:	None
Compiled by:	The Federal Reserve District Banks
Frequency:	Eight times per year
Release date:	Two weeks preceding the Fed's FOMC meeting
Published data:	*The Beige Book*, The Federal Reserve Board of Governors
Internet:	http://www.federalreserve.gov/
	http://www.EconSources.com

---

[18] Fettig, et al. "The Federal Reserve's Beige Book," *The Region*, 1999. This article describes both studies in more detail.

Chapter 7

PRICES, MONEY, and INTEREST RATES

Consumer Price Index

The consumer price index, or CPI, is one of the most comprehensive statistical measures compiled by the Bureau of Labor Statistics. In fact, the BLS actually computes two measures. The first, and most important, is the ***CPI for all urban consumers (CPI-U)***, which covers about 89 percent of the total population. The second, which overlaps the first, is the ***CPI for urban wage earners and clerical workers (CPI-W)*** and covers about 28 percent of the population. CPI data are released about two weeks after the close of the reference month.

Each index is a measure of the average change in prices for a fixed "market basket" of goods and services used by consumers. It is not, however, the same as a cost-of-living index because it does not take into account all of the factors that would allow one to maintain the same standard of living with a given level of expenditures.[1]

Constructing the Sample

The CPI uses a market basket of goods and services that most consumers typically buy. From this, the BLS constructed a list of eight

---

[1] Missing from the analysis are such things as the impact of government regulations, environmental factors, and even matters like crime, health, and water quality. When asked by a Congressional advisory committee to establish a cost-of-living index as the primary objective of the CPI, the BLS response was that "if the BLS staff or other technical experts knew how to produce a true cost-or-living index on a monthly production schedule, that would be what we would produce." See "Consumer Price Indexes: Short Term Recommendations," 1998 CPI Revisions BLS website.

Table 7-1

Major Product Groups and Entry Level Sampling Items in the CPI

PG#1. Food and Beverages

      EC#1: Cereals and bakery products

          Strata #1: Cereals and cereal products

              ELI#1: *Flour and prepared flour mixes*

              ELI#2: *Breakfast cereal*

              ELI#3: *Rice, pasta, cornmeal*

          Strata #2: Bakery products

              ELI#1: *Bread*

              ELI#1: *Fresh biscuits, rolls, muffins*

              ELI#1: *Cakes, cupcakes, and cookies*

              ELI#2: *Other bakery products*

      EC#2: Meats, poultry, fish and eggs

        ....

PG#2. Housing

PG#3. Apparel

PG#4. Transportation

PG#5. Medical Care

PG#6. Recreation

PG#7. Education and Communication

PG#8. Other Goods and Services

Source: *Consumer Price Index News Release*, BLS, March 2017

major product groups (PGs) which were broken down into approximately 70 expenditure classes (ECs), more than 200 strata, and over 300 entry level items (ELIs) in the manner illustrated in Table 7-1.

Each of the 70,000+ sampled items is then priced and repriced at regular monthly intervals. Because the final dollar value of market basket would be so large, the new market basket prices are expressed as a percent of 1982–84 base period prices.[2] To illustrate, a CPI of 245.030 in August 2017 means that the market basket amounted to 245.030 percent of its base period cost, or that an

---

[2] The choice of a base year is not that important because comparisons between any two years can be found by simply dividing two values of the CPI. For example, if the CPI in April 2016 was 239.261, and if the CPI in April 2007 was 206.686, then April 2016 prices were 239.261/206.686 = 1.158, or 1.158 times higher than they were nine years earlier. Alternatively, we could say that prices increased by 15.8 percent over the same period. This can be done for any other years.

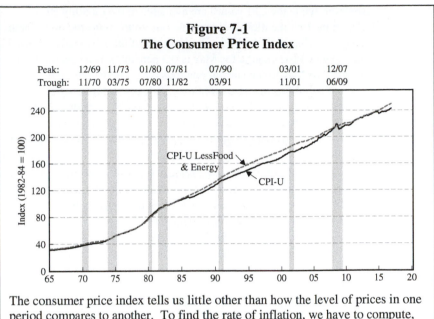

Figure 7-1
The Consumer Price Index

| Peak: | 12/69 | 11/73 | 01/80 | 07/81 | 07/90 | | 03/01 | 12/07 |
| Trough: | 11/70 | 03/75 | 07/80 | 11/82 | 03/91 | | 11/01 | 06/09 |

The consumer price index tells us little other than how the level of prices in one period compares to another. To find the rate of inflation, we have to compute, and then annualize monthly changes in the CPI.

item costing $1 in the 1982–84 base period would cost $2.45 in August 2017.

When we observe the CPI-U over time, as in Figure 7-1, it seems to have little relationship to the expansions and contractions of the economy. At best, we could say that the CPI-U appears to rise in the latter stage of an expansion, and then falters or even contracts during a recession. Another measure in the figure is the so-called CPI "core" that does not include the more volatile food and energy price categories. Because the "core" CPI-U is more stable than the CPI-U, is seems to almost always go up, even during a recession as severe as the Great Recession of 2008–09.

Major Uses of the CPI

The CPI can be thought of as the level of prices, which has the three main uses:

- **As an indicator of inflation:** If the CPI has a value of 201.800 in one year and 202.416 in the next, the 0.616 point change in the index is a 0.616/201.800 = 0.003, for an annual inflation rate of 0.3 percent.

However, while the CPI values are available in the monthly BLS release, the first mention is always the *seasonally adjusted* one-month percentage change in the CPI. For example, if the seasonally adjusted one-month CPI-U change for May is 0.3 percent, it is measured from the previous May to the current one thus covering the previous 12-months.[3] When the next monthly CPI-U percentage change is issued, it will again be for the previous 12 months, only this time covering June to June. This is the most widely reported measure of inflation and is shown in Figure 7-2 along with the CPI-U core rate of inflation.

- **As a deflator of other economic series:** Suppose we wanted to know if the real purchasing power of the minimum wage changed between 1996 when it was $4.75/hr. and 2016 when it was $7.25/hr. To do so, we divide the wage in each year by the CPI in those years to deflate both values. This gives us ($4.75/156.9)(100) = $3.03 for 1996, and ($7.25/240.007)(100) = $3.02 for 2016, so the deflated values tell us that the real purchasing power of the minimum wage was essentially the same in both 1996 and 2016.[4]

- **As a means of adjusting dollar values:** According to the BLS, "Over 50 million social security beneficiaries, and military and Federal Civil Service retirees, have cost-of-living adjustments tied to the CPI."[5] Increases in the CPI are also used to adjust the marginal tax brackets in the federal income tax code to prevent inflation induced increases in tax rates—sometimes known as "bracket creep."

The Historical Record

The inflation rate shown in Figure 7-2 generally increases during the latter part of an expansion and then, with the exception of

---

[3] Seasonally adjusted values are preferred to unadjusted ones which are distorted by seasonal influences such as weather, harvest, production cycles, sales, model changeovers, or other seasonal factors that normally occur annually. Seasonally adjusted numbers remove these distortions and make monthly comparisons of annual inflation rates less volatile.

[4] The two results, $3.03 and $3.02, *bear absolutely no relationship to anything other than to each other*. Note that the "times 100" in the computation was necessary because the CPI itself is a percent of prices in the 1982–84 base year. If a CPI of 156.9 percent in 1996 is the same as 1.569, we could have divided $4.75 by 1.569 to get the same $3.03 result. As for the use of three decimals for the CPI, the BLS began publishing CPI indices in three places as of January 2007; prior to that only one decimal place was used.

[5] *CPI Frequently Asked Questions (FAQs)*, https://www.bls.gov/cpi/cpifaq.htm, updated February 1, 2017.

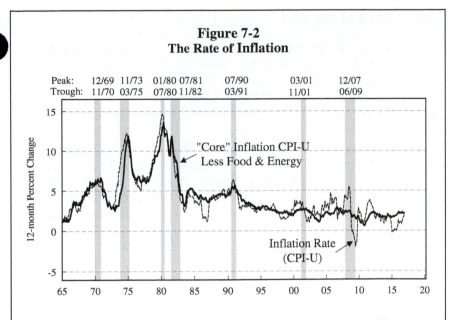

Figure 7-2
The Rate of Inflation

Peak: 12/69 11/73   01/80 07/81   07/90   03/01   12/07
Trough: 11/70 03/75   07/80 11/82   03/91   11/01   06/09

The annual rate of inflation is determined by annualizing seasonally adjusted changes in the CPI-U. The "core" rate of inflation, or the CPI-U less food and energy prices, is slightly more stable than the overall inflation rate.

the Great Recession of 2008–09, begins to decline during a recession. While the CPI-U inflation series has been relatively stable since the mid-1980s, it has no particular value as a leading indicator of recessions or economic recoveries.

Despite all of the attention given to one-month percentage changes in the CPI-U, the BLS is reluctant to define it as the "best" measure of inflation. Instead it says that the CPI measures inflation only experienced by consumers while the Producer Price Index (PPI), the Employment Cost Index (ECI), the BLS International Price Program, and the Gross Domestic Product Deflator (GDP deflator) are all used to measure inflation covering different segments of the economy.[6]

---

[6] *CPI Frequently Asked Questions (FAQs)*, https://www.bls.gov/bls/faqs.htm, updated July 6, 2016.

The Politics of the CPI

Because of the enormous impact of the CPI, it is constantly under scrutiny.   One instance was in 1996 when a special Congressional commission reported that the measure overestimated the annual cost of living by nearly 1.1 percent.[7] At the time, the main culprit was the fixed market basket which had not been updated since 1982–1984.

The commission also reported that a 1-percentage point annual reduction in the CPI would reduce the federal deficit by about $1 trillion over 12 years—savings due to lower cost-of-living payments to social security recipients, higher receipts from taxpayers as personal income tax bracket adjustments become smaller, and lower costs of other federal programs that are indexed to the CPI. This, of course, added a political element to the revision especially as the Federal government was struggling to balance its budget at the time.

The problem, now fixed, was that the market basket did not account for the substitution effects that occur when consumers use one product rather than another, nor did it take into account changes in shopping patterns that occur when consumers shop at discount outlets. Finally, quality improvements to existing products such as VCRs and computers tended to get overlooked.[8]

The BLS did address some other methodological issues, and the CPI is better for it. Even so, the CPI today is neither more nor less than it ever was: a measure of the average change over time in the prices paid by urban consumers for a market basket of consumer goods and services.

A Price Index Just for Christmas?

A humorous take on the application of a price index is the PNC's Christmas Price Index which estimates the annual price of each gift in the popular seasonal song, "The Twelve Days of Christmas."

---

[7] *Final report of the advisory commission to study the Consumer Price Index* (The Boskin Commission Report), U.S. Senate Committee on Finance, December 1996.

[8] A comprehensive annotated chronology of changes in the Consumer Price Index can be found in "The Consumer Price Index (Updated 06/2015)" *BLS Handbook of Methods*, Chapter 17, pp. 8-10.

The series provides a whimsical, if somewhat dubious, look at annual Christmas gift price changes occurring in the 12 days of Christmas song since 1984.

And, for Christmas 2016 the total price index went up by 0.7 percent, a change largely due to an increase in the price of turtle doves which happened to be in short supply.[9]

Who said economic statistics can't be fun?

The Consumer Price Index

Indicator status:	None
Compiled by:	Bureau of Labor Statistics
Frequency:	Monthly
Release date:	8th through 19th of the following month
Revisions:	Seasonal revisions in January for up to 5 years
Published data:	*Economic Indicators*, Council of Economic Advisors
	News Release, Consumer Price Index, Bureau of Labor Statistics
Internet:	https://www.bls.gov/cpi/
	http://www.EconSources.com

---

[9] https://www.pnc.com/en/about-pnc/topics/pnc-christmas-price-index.html

Producer Price Index

Another important price series is the ***producer price index (PPI)***, which measures average changes in selling prices received by domestic producers for their output. Until 1978, the series was known as the *wholesale price index*, but the title was changed to emphasize the fact that only price changes between the producer and the *first* purchaser of the product were covered. It does not measure price changes that occur between other intermediaries such as the final wholesaler and the retailer who buys the product for resale to the public.

Coverage and Reporting

Every month, over 100,000 price quotations are obtained from roughly 25,000 establishments representing practically every sector of the U.S. economy. The PPI survey covers virtually all of the goods manufacturing sector and approximately three quarters of service industry sector. Price indices are then prepared for three major groups: final demand-intermediate demand (FD-ID), commodity indexes, and net industry and product indexes.[10]

Final PPI reports are made available for more than 10,000 individual products and product groups. Because of this, the BLS likes to think of the PPI as a "family of indexes" measuring price changes over time for domestically produced goods, services, and construction.[11]

The most recent change in the PPI occurred during the January 2014 transition to FD-ID. The Final Demand component of the survey reports on sales of finished goods for personal consumption, capital investment, government purchase, and export. The Intermediate Demand component of the survey reports on final prices producers receive when their goods or services are sold as inputs to other businesses. The FD-ID structure allows for the tracking of a product's price increase as it moves through the stages of production to its final end use.

---

[10] "Technical Notes" *Producer Price Index News Release*, Bureau of Labor Statistics, March 2017.

[11] For an interesting history of the PPI see Lana Conforti, "The First 50 Years of the Producer Price Index: setting inflation expectations for today," Monthly Labor Review, U.S. Bureau of Labor Statistics, June 2016 https://DOI.org/MLR.10.21916.25.

The Historical Record

Figure 7-3 shows the PPI for finished goods, one of the main summary statistics in the PPI family of indices, along with the CPI-U. The two series were relatively close until about 1985, after which the PPI fell behind and became considerably more volatile.   Still, increases in the PPI eventually cause increases in the CPI-U because if prices go up at the factory, consumers will certainly pay more later on.   Some of this relationship between a rising PPI and increases in the CPI are evident in Figure 7-3.

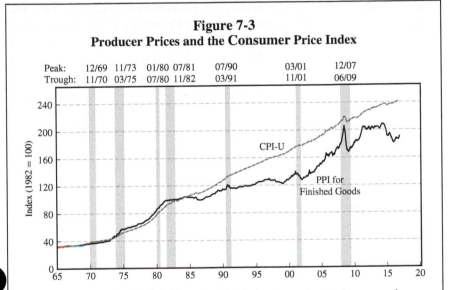

Figure 7-3
Producer Prices and the Consumer Price Index

The PPI has not kept pace with the CPI in recent years, in part because of differences in coverage between the two series and in part due to structural changes in the economy. Still, the PPI is still thought of as a precursor to a rise in consumer prices. It has no other status as an economic indicator.

Other Uses of the PPI

Other uses for the PPI are fairly technical. For example, PPI data are used by the Bureau of Economic Analysis to deflate domestic revenue streams to get better estimates of real GDP growth. PPI data are also used for escalator clauses in long-term contracts. A cereal producer tied to a long-term supply contract may have a clause that will adjust its final contract value upward if there is an unexpected increase in the price of an input such as wheat or sugar. Or, a producer of specialized petroleum products may have an escalator clause that will adjust the final contract price of its output if there is an unexpected change in petroleum prices.

Still, one of the main uses of the PPI is that it provides an additional indicator of inflation that complements the CPI. This is because the two measures sample different parts of the economy. The PPI covers the entire market output of U.S. producers whereas the CPI only includes prices of several hundred products commonly purchased by consumers. The CPI includes imports whereas the PPI does not. The CPI includes imputed values for homeowner rents whereas the PPI does not. The PPI covers government purchases whereas the CPI does not. Finally, the PPI covers sales to businesses if the sales are used for capital investment, whereas the CPI does not.[12]

Clearly, a more accurate view of overall inflation may well require the observer to consider changes in the PPI along with changes in the CPI.

Producer Price Index	
Indicator status:	No indicator of changes in real GDP
Compiled by:	Bureau of Labor Statistics
Frequency:	Monthly
Release date:	Second week of the following month
Revisions:	Up to four months after the initial monthly release
Published data:	*PPI News Release*, Bureau of Labor Statistics
	Economic Indicators, Council of Economic Advisors
Internet:	https://www.bls.gov/ppi/

---

[12] *Producer Price Index, Frequently Asked Questions (FAQs)*, Updated October 15, 2015, https://www.bls.gov/ppi/ppifaq.htm

Money Supply

Economists like to think of money as anything that serves as a unit of account, a medium of exchange, and a store of value. However, an exact measurement of the money stock is complicated by the fact that it takes so many different forms, ranging from coins to savings accounts to Eurodollar deposits.[13]

Definitions of Money

The Fed employs several definitions of money, two of which correspond to the functions of money described above.[14] One is called *M1* and is the transactional component of the money supply, or the part most closely identified with money's role as a medium of exchange. As can be seen in Table 7-2, this definition of the money supply includes coins, paper currency, traveler's checks, demand deposits, NOW accounts, credit union share drafts, and other checkable deposits.

Table 7-2
Components of the Money Supply, Billions of Dollars

1. Coins, paper currency outside the U.S. Treasury & the Fed	$1,446.1
2. Traveler's checks issued by nonbanks	2.1
3. Demand deposits at commercial banks	1,428.2
4. Other checkable deposits (NOW accounts, share drafts)	561.3
M1	**$3,437.7**
5. Savings deposits	
(includes money market deposit accounts)	8,923.1
6. Small denomination time deposits (less than $100,000)	342.7
7. Retail money market mutual funds	677.0
M2 = (M1 plus lines 5–7)	**$13,380.5**

Source: *Statistical Release H.6*, May 4, 2017, Federal Reserve Board of Governors

If we want to consider money's role as a store of value as well as a medium of exchange, the definition is expanded to include other,

---

[13] Dollar-denominated bank deposits in foreign countries, not necessarily in Europe.

[14] Four definitions—M1, M2, M3, and DEBT—had been used by the Fed. However, the current *Money Stock and Debt Measures H.6 Release* only reports M1 and M2.

and sometimes lesser known, forms of holding money. This broader-based definition of money is known as *M2*, and we get it by adding savings deposits (including money market deposit accounts), small-denomination time deposits, and retail money market mutual funds to M1. These seven different components of M1 and M2 are shown in Table 7-2.

The Historical Record

Since the Federal Reserve System manages the size of the money supply in order to control the interest rate, we would expect that variations in the money stock occur over time. Accordingly, the levels of M1 and M2 are plotted in Figure 7-4 from 1965 to the present. According to the figure, M1 has risen steadily since 2009, and M2 has risen steadily since approximately 1996. And, aside from a short burst of growth during the Great Recession of 2008–09, neither series seems to have affected, or been affected by, changes in overall economic activity.

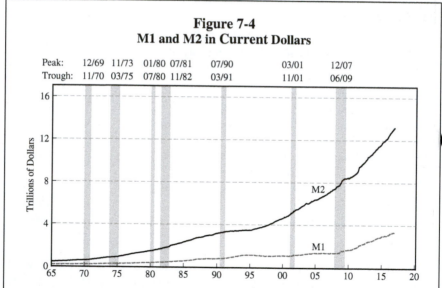

Figure 7-4
M1 and M2 in Current Dollars

| Peak: | 12/69 | 11/73 | 01/80 | 07/81 | 07/90 | | 03/01 | | 12/07 |
| Trough: | 11/70 | 03/75 | 07/80 | 11/82 | 03/91 | | 11/01 | | 06/09 |

Although a variation of M2 had once been considered a leading indicator of recessions, economists now worry that the excessive monetary expansion since the Great Recession of 2008–09 will be a factor causing inflation to return.

Is Money a Leading Economic Indicator?

It turns out that money, like any other commodity, can also be measured in terms of current or constant dollar amounts, the latter being preferable if we want to compensate for the distortions of inflation. If the two series shown in Figure 7-4 were converted to constant dollar amounts, they would both exhibit some modest leading indicator characteristics. In fact, M2 in constant dollars had historically been included in The Conference Board's *Leading Economic Index (LEI)* although it is no longer used.[15]

The process of converting M1 or M2 to constant dollar measures is not difficult, but it is not done by the Fed—which is the reason that only current dollar amounts are shown here. Instead, the Fed only reports its money statistics in current terms, leaving the conversion to others.[16]

If anything, the sharp increase in both monetary measures during and after 2008–09 reflects the Fed's aggressive monetary policies during that period. Finally, we should also mention that extensive studies by monetarists have found a strong, if somewhat delayed and irregular, link between changes in the level of M2 and the price level. Because of this, we need to keep an eye on M2 growth since it may indicate a resumption of future inflation and higher interest rates.

M1 and M2	
Indicator status:	Both series: no value as indicators of recession or recovery
Compiled by:	Federal Reserve Board of Governors
Frequency:	Weekly
Release date:	4:30 p.m. Thursdays for the previous week
Revisions:	None
Published data:	*Statistical Release H.6*, Fed Board of Governors
	Federal Reserve Bulletin, Fed Board of Governors
Internet:	http://www.federalreserve.gov
	http://www.EconSources.com

---

[15] The list of component series that make up the *LEI* is in Table 3-1 on page 51.

[16] One way to make the conversion is to divide M2 by the implicit price deflator for personal consumption expenditures, and then multiply it by 100.

Fed Funds Rate

Fed funds are excess reserve balances that banks and other financial institutions lend to one another on a short-term basis. The interest paid to borrow these funds is known as the *federal funds rate*. Most loans are overnight, although some may be for as long as three days. However, the federal funds rate is most important because it's the rate targeted by the Fed's Federal Open Market Committee (FOMC) when it executes monetary policy.

A Short History of Fed Funds

Historically, member banks of the Federal Reserve System were required to keep deposits at the Fed as reserves against savings accounts and checking deposits. Because the Fed did not pay interest on these reserves, member banks had little incentive to keep more funds than they needed. But if a bank had excess reserves, it would often lend the surplus to another member bank on an overnight or weekend basis for a modest fee. Banks that borrowed the excess reserves often did so to shore up their own reserves at the Fed.

When the loans were made, the funds never really left the Fed—hence the term "fed" in the title. All a member bank needed to do to make a transaction was to notify its district Fed bank that reserve funds were to be transferred from its account to another bank's account for a short period of time, after which the funds would be transferred back. Today the market for fed funds is far more sophisticated and is dominated by brokers who facilitate transfers.[17]

Over time, federal funds took on a more generic meaning as the practice of borrowing one another's reserves expanded to financial institutions outside the Federal Reserve System.[18] Today, financial institutions deal with one another through the Fed since all depository institutions have access.

---

[17] The daily effective fed funds rate is a weighted average of rates on trades through N.Y. brokers. Rates are annualized using a 360-day year.

[18] Nonmember state banks, for example, might lend reserves to one another under this system.

00-00-.

A Leading Indicator

The history of the federal funds rate since 1965 is presented in Figure 7-5. Like many other interest rates in the economy, in recent years it has tended to act as a leading indicator for peaks in overall economic activity. This pattern is probably due to the Fed's proactive role in trying to prevent or at least mitigate economic downturns. For example, if the economy shows signs of slowing or entering a recession, the Fed may lower the rate to encourage banks to borrow and create excess reserves that will enable them to increase lending.

The Fed is also likely to keep the rate low until the recovery is well underway, so the fed funds rate does not begin to turn up until well after the recession has ended—making the series a lagging indicator for recoveries.

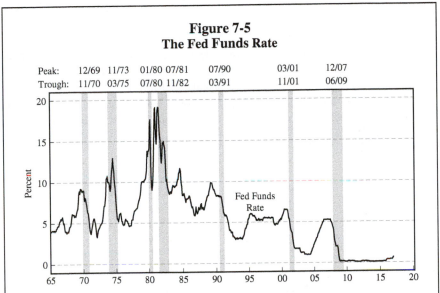

Figure 7-5
The Fed Funds Rate

| Peak: | 12/69 | 11/73 | 01/80 07/81 | 07/90 | 03/01 | 12/07 |
| Trough: | 11/70 | 03/75 | 07/80 11/82 | 03/91 | 11/01 | 06/09 |

Fed funds are short-term reserves that banks and other financial institutions lend to each other overnight, or for a few days at a time. The fed funds rate is the rate of interest that the FOMC targets when it executes monetary policy.

Pushing on a String

If the Fed has a problem with using the fed funds rate as an instrument of monetary policy, it's that commercial banks may not increase their lending even if the Fed successfully increases their excess reserves. After all, borrowers, like investors and potential homeowners, can only be encouraged to borrow, they cannot be forced. This is why economists say that executing monetary policy is sometimes like "pushing on a string." Pulling on a string (or increasing interest rates) may work—but pushing on a string, not so much so.

Figure 7-5 also shows another limitation of monetary policy, and that is that interest rates can only go so low. The post-2009 fed funds rate in the figure is clearly at a historic low, and if another recession were to have occurred in 2017, it would have been difficult to decrease the rate much further. Of course economists were pleased that the Fed worked so aggressively to stimulate economic growth during and after the Great Recession of 2008–09, but when the rate is as close to zero as it was between 2009 and 2016, it's about as low as it can go.

Then again, maybe zero is not as low as interest rates can go. After all, Sweden's Riksbank, the Danish National Bank, the Swiss National Bank, the Bank of Japan and the European Central Bank have recently experimented with negative interest rates. To reduce real borrowing costs below zero, the lender (the Fed) would have to pay the borrower (a commercial bank) to borrow funds rather than the other way around. The mechanics are more complicated than this, but it could happen.

Fed Funds Rate	
Indicator status:	Leading for recessions; lagging for recoveries
Compiled by:	Federal Reserve Board of Governors
Frequency:	Daily
Release date:	Daily
Revisions:	None
Published data:	*Federal Reserve Bulletin*, Fed Board of Governors
	Statistical Release H.15, Fed Board of Governors
Internet:	https://www.federalreserve.gov/
	http://www.EconSources.com

Primary Credit Rate

In its central bank role as a "lender of last resort," the Federal Reserve System is expected to lend funds to other financial institutions, especially in times of need. Historically, the Fed used the term *discount rate* to designate the interest rate on short-term borrowed funds that commercial banks could receive when they brought bills of credit to the Fed for discounting.

However, today the term "discount rate" is a misnomer because virtually all loans made by the Fed are in the form of advances rather than discounts. In addition, for much of its history the discount rate was not even a competitive rate—it was instead a policy tool used to control the money supply and influence the general level of interest rates.[19]

From Discount to Primary Credit

When the Fed was established in 1913, the discount rate was intended to be the primary tool of monetary policy. The idea was that borrowers would bring "real" bills of credit—short-term IOUs backed by inventories and other real assets—to the Fed for discount. The borrowed funds would temporarily expand the money supply, and when the bills reached maturity and were repaid, the money supply would contract. The process was designed to make the money supply "elastic" in the sense that it would expand when businesses needed additional funds to convert inventories into finished products, and then contract when the additional funds were not needed.

Before long, however, the Fed discovered it could also buy and sell government bonds to manage the money supply and affect changes in interest rates, a function now performed by the Federal Open Market Committee (FOMC) when it targets the fed funds rate. It may seem redundant to have an independently administered primary credit rate coexist with the FOMC's targeted fed funds rate, but this arrangement had two advantages for the Fed. First, the discount rate was set in conjunction with the district Fed banks, a requirement of

---

[19] *Discount Window Lending Programs Frequently Asked Questions (FAQs)*, May 2017, https://www.frbdiscountwindow.org/en/Frequently_Asked_Questions.aspx.

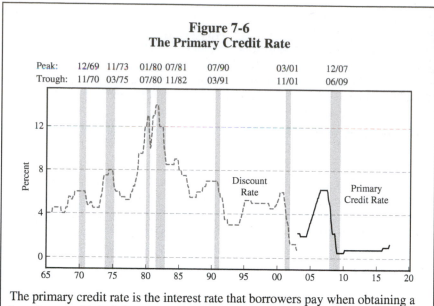

Figure 7-6
The Primary Credit Rate

| Peak: | 12/69 | 11/73 | 01/80 07/81 | 07/90 | 03/01 | 12/07 |
| Trough: | 11/70 | 03/75 | 07/80 11/82 | 03/91 | 11/01 | 06/09 |

The primary credit rate is the interest rate that borrowers pay when obtaining a loan from the Fed. It is a tool of monetary policy and therefore not especially responsive to the broader forces of supply and demand for loanable funds.

the Federal Reserve Act.[20]   Second, it generated an "announcement effect" which served as a source of policy information for Fed watchers.

In January 2003, the Fed introduced the ***primary credit rate*** shown in Figure 7-6 as the successor to the discount rate. The main purpose of the new primary credit program was to introduce flexibility so that short-term credit could be made available as a backup liquidity source to generally sound financial institutions. Simultaneously, the Fed gave up its discretionary authority to reject discount rate loans in circumstances deemed inconsistent with sound banking practices.

Under the new primary credit rate policy no questions are asked about, and no restrictions imposed on, the use of the borrowed funds.

---

[20] The Federal Reserve Act requires the board of directors in the 12 district Fed banks determine the discount rate in their district, subject to final approval by the Fed's Board of Governors. For an interesting description of this process, see E. Jay Stevens, "Setting the Discount Rate," *Economic Commentary*, Federal Reserve Bank of Cleveland, July 15, 1989.

In return, the primary funds rate is allowed to fluctuate modestly above the targeted fed funds rate at the discretion of the Fed. And, if a borrowing institution is not eligible for primary credit, it can apply for "secondary credit" at a slightly higher cost. All borrowing is still done at the Fed's discount window, but the revamped policies in 2003 generally make discount window borrowing more flexible.

The Historical Record

Figure 7-6 shows the history of the discount and primary credit rates from 1965 to the present. Because the primary credit rate is no longer an administered rate, but was determined largely by the forces of supply and demand, it behaved more like a leading indicator for the Great Recession of 2008–09.

Whether or not that pattern persists may well depend upon the timing of the next recession. After all, the primary credit rate, like the fed funds rate, was also near its historic low in 2016. If a recession were to have occurred in 2017 or shortly thereafter, it would have been difficult for the rate to go low enough to reliably predict an impending recession.

Primary Credit Rate	
Indicator status:	Leading indicator for recessions
Compiled by:	Federal Reserve Board of Governors
Frequency:	Daily
Release date:	Daily
Revisions:	None
Published data:	*Federal Reserve Bulletin*, Fed Board of Governors
	Statistical Release H.15, Fed Board of Governors
Internet:	https://www.federalreserve.gov/
	http://www.EconSources.com

Treasury Bill Rate

The *Treasury bill rate* is one of the most important short-term interest rates in the economy. Treasury bills (T-bills) are popular with investors because they are auctioned weekly and traded daily.[21] They are also popular because they are among the safest of all possible investments. As a result, the rate on T-bills reflects the most current market forces of supply and demand.

The Historical Record

The history of T-bill rates appears in Figure 7-7, along with the discount and primary credit rates for comparison purposes. Perhaps the most remarkable thing about the figure is that the T-bill rate reached during and after the Great Recession of 2008–09 was so historically low.

The level of T-bill rates during and after 2009 is a testament to the Fed's ability to achieve low interest rates. The influence of the discount/primary credit rate on T-bills is clearly evident as the T-bill rate was pushed to 0.19 percent in January 2009. Shortly thereafter, T-bill rates went even lower to 0.02 percent and did not begin to recover until early 2016 when rates inched up to 0.31 percent.

Why T-bill Rates Matter

T-bills are issued by the U.S. Treasury whenever the government deficit spends—which is to say on an all-to-regular basis. In fact, the government simply couldn't operate without the constant stream of funds that investors, both domestic and foreign, willingly lend the government. T-bills may make up slightly less than 10 percent of total

---

[21] A Treasury bill is a short-term obligation with a maturity of 13, 26, or 52 weeks. T-bills have minimum denominations of $10,000 and do not pay interest directly because they are sold on a discount basis. For example, an investor may purchase a 52-week bill for $9,300. The $700 difference between the amount paid and the amount received at maturity is the investor's profit. The $700 return on the $9,300 investment is a yield of $700/$9,300 = 0.0753, or 7.53 percent.

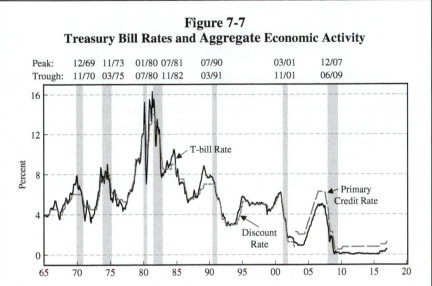

Figure 7-7
Treasury Bill Rates and Aggregate Economic Activity

Peak:	12/69	11/73	01/80 07/81	07/90		03/01	12/07
Trough:	11/70	03/75	07/80 11/82	03/91		11/01	06/09

The T-bill rate is one of the most competitive rates in the economy and a good indicator of changes in the supply and demand for funds. T-bills are popular with investors because they are the safest of all possible investments.

U.S. Treasury securities outstanding, but even minuscule changes in rates can mean a difference of hundreds of millions of dollars to both borrowers and investors.[22] Perhaps that's why they watch the rate so closely.

Treasury Bill Rate	
Indicator status:	Leading for recessions; lagging for recoveries
Compiled by:	Federal Reserve Board of Governors
Frequency:	Daily
Release date:	Daily
Published data:	*Federal Reserve Bulletin*, Fed Board of Governors
	Statistical Release H.15, Fed Board of Governors
Internet:	https://www.federalreserve.gov/
	http://www.EconSources.com

---

[22] *Monthly Statement of the Public Debt of the United States,* April 30, 2017, https://treasurydirect.gov/govt/reports/

Prime Rate

Historically, the ***prime rate*** was the rate banks charged their best customers. Because of this, it received wide publicity as the lowest rate available from banks. Things have changed since then, and so the prime rate today is not quite the same as it used to be. Despite these changes, it is still widely watched.

If You Get the Prime Rate, Do You Actually Pay It?

That depends. Suppose a business borrows $100,000 at a 10 percent prime rate. However, the company may not get to use all the funds because the bank may require a *compensating balance*, or a deposit (usually interest free), in the amount of $5000. On a simple interest basis, the company is really paying $10,000 for the use of $95,000, which computes to a 10.53 percent simple rate.

Another bank may have an identical prime but a different compensating balance requirement in the amount of $9000 per $100,000 borrowed. A borrower at this bank would still pay 10 percent on the $100,000 for an interest cost of $10,000 but have access to only $91,000, for a 10.99 percent simple rate.

The Historical Record

The Fed determines the predominant prime rate by surveying the 25 largest banks in the country according to total asset size.[23] The predominant prime is the rate that most of the banks in the sample use. Once the predominant prime is established, the Fed waits for the majority of the banks to adopt a new rate before the prime is recomputed.

The prime rate illustrated in Figure 7-8 appears to adjust in stages. That is, it stays at one level for a time before adjusting to a new one. There are two reasons for this. First, the official prime rate

---

[23] The 25 largest banks are determined by the Fed's weekly call report. As a result, while the majority of the largest banks in the list remain relatively constant, mergers and other occurrences can change the sample's membership.

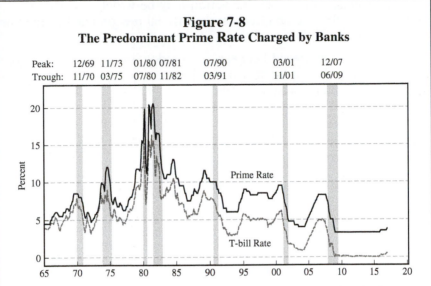

Figure 7-8
The Predominant Prime Rate Charged by Banks

Peak:	12/69	11/73	01/80 07/81	07/90		03/01	12/07
Trough:	11/70	03/75	07/80 11/82	03/91		11/01	06/09

This series is sometimes called the "average" prime rate charged by banks, but it's not an average. If 13 banks in the Fed sample charge a prime rate of 7 percent, and if the remaining 12 charge 9 percent, the predominant prime will be 7 percent.

compiled by the Fed represents the *prevailing* level—meaning the rate charged by the largest number of banks in the sample—rather than an average of the rates charged by all banks. Second, banks are more inclined to change the compensating balance requirement rather than the prime, especially if interest rates are rising.

What Does a Change in the Prime Tell Us?

Not much actually. Because banks can increase effective interest rates by changing the compensating balance, a change in the prime generally indicates that changes in the economy have already taken place, and that the prime is just adjusting to the new reality.

As an economic indicator of future changes in GDP, the prime is a coincident indicator for recessions and a lagging indicator for recoveries. Changes in the prime rate may make headlines, but the changes normally reflect other interest rate adjustments that have already taken place. Occasionally, a prominent bank not on the list of

25 may change its rate, and the action may be widely reported in the press, but it will have no effect on the official predominant prime rate compiled by the Fed.

Finally, the spread between the predominant prime and T-bill rates is simply due to the fact that a business borrower has a greater risk of default than does the government.

Prime Rate	
Indicator status:	Coincident recessions, lagging for recoveries
Compiled by:	Federal Reserve Board of Governors
Frequency:	Daily
Release date:	Daily
Revisions:	None
Published data:	*Federal Reserve Bulletin*, Fed Board of Governors
	Statistical Release H.15, Fed Board of Governors
Internet:	https://www.federalreserve.gov/
	http://www.EconSources.com

The Libor

The *Libor*, or *London Interbank Offer Rate*, was and perhaps still is the world's most prestigious and widely used benchmark to determine short-term interest rates—although it hit a major speedbump in 2012. Originally it was the rate of interest that banks charged when they loaned money to each other in the London wholesale money markets. Because of subsequent manipulations however, an ensuing scandal was said to have "dwarf[ed] by orders of magnitude any financial scam in the history of markets."[24]

By 2012 Libor was used in more than $300 *trillion* of contracts involving derivatives, loans, and mortgages. While it had a global reach, it also had a major stronghold in U.S. markets. For example, by 2008 alone, billions of dollars of interest rate swaps, an esoteric financial derivative, were indexed to the Libor at the Chicago Mercantile Exchange. In the same year it was estimated that about 40 percent of all prime loans and up to 90 percent of all subprime mortgages in the state of Ohio alone were indexed to the Libor rate.

But, how did the Libor get its start and how should we think about it now?

Why London?

The story starts in London when an enterprising Greek banker by the name of Minos Zombanakis was working on a way to benchmark international short-term interest rates that would be simple, fair, universally accepted, and free from abuse or manipulation by government regulatory bodies or unscrupulous traders. At the time, London was awash with U.S. dollars that Russia, China, and some Gulf states did not want to deposit in the United States for fear of possible confiscation. As a result, Eurodollar deposits[25]

---

[24] Andrew Lo, MIT Professor of Finance, The LIBOR Scandal Explained, http://www.accountingdegree.net/, 2012.

[25] Dollar-denominated bank deposits in foreign countries, but not necessarily in Europe.

became popular and multibillion Eurodollar loans were being made internationally.[26]

The idea was to convince a group of syndicated banks to periodically share their lowest expected interest rate funding costs for new and renewing loans. A small margin for profit would be added to the average of the reported rates, and the result would be the "benchmarked" interest rate for the next loan period.

How Was It Determined?

The scheme worked well at first, but banks normally make new loans daily and the dollar was not the only international currency traded in London. As the daily computational requirements of the Libor became more demanding, the British Bankers Association offered to administer it.[27]   After consultations with the Bank of England, the only major change to the original formula was to rank the daily interest rate submissions from highest to lowest and then eliminate the top and bottom quarters leaving the remainder to be averaged as the new benchmark.

The procedure then became fairly routine. Just before 11:00 a.m., the BBA would conduct a daily survey of approximately 15 of the largest commercial banks in the London wholesale market. Each bank in the survey would be asked to provide the lowest rate they expected to pay if they were to borrow or exchange currencies from other commercial banks.   These data were collected for a number of currencies and maturities, and the resulting rates were published at about 11:30 a.m. The rates then remained unchanged until they were reestablished again the next day.

Because the banks were large competitive institutions, and because the foreign currencies and Eurodollars that they lent each other were outside the control of the Federal Reserve System, the Libor rate was thought to be generally free of political and regulatory influence.

Figure 7-9 presents the BBA's Libor from its inception in January 1986 along with the American T-bill rate. The two rates

---

[26] For a fascinating and comprehensive discussion of the Libor, see The Fix: How Bankers Lied, Cheated and Colluded to Rig the World's Most Important Number, Wiley, December 2016, by Gavin Finch and Liam Vaughan, award-winning financial crime reporters for Bloomberg News in London.

[27] The BBA is a nonprofit trade association.

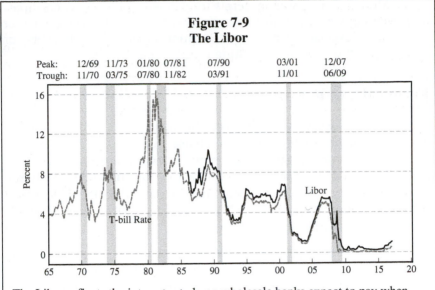

Figure 7-9
The Libor

Peak: 12/69 11/73 01/80 07/81   07/90   03/01   12/07
Trough: 11/70 03/75 07/80 11/82   03/91   11/01   06/09

The Libor reflects the interest rate large wholesale banks expect to pay when borrowing dollars from each other. It is established daily from a survey of approximately 15 large commercial banks.

follow each other fairly closely, although the Libor was usually the slightly higher of the two at any given time. Everything was running smoothly until the Libor diverged significantly from other interest rates just before the Great Recession of 2008–09.

What Went Wrong?

Although some indications of manipulation occurred prior to the financial crisis of 2008, more serious revelations of misconduct did not surface until 2011 and 2012. A series of investigations on both sides of the Atlantic quickly followed and uncovered substantial problems. For example, banks sometimes submitted the same interest rate day after day while others did not. In one instance, JP Morgan Chase reported a 1 percent loan rate for every day during June 2012 while UBS, another major bank in the Libor, had a different rate that changed daily and was calculated to three decimal places.[28]

---

[28] "Libor Scandal Shows Many Flaws in Rate-Setting" *New York Times*, July 20, 2012.

More damning were excerpts from emails, phone conversations, and even conversations in public forums that caught bankers either requesting favorable Libor quotes from other Libor bankers or admitting that they were submitting incorrect data.

From BBA to ICE

The outrage over the biggest "financial scam in the history of markets" was both immediate and intense. In June 2012, the British government commissioned a report recommending that the administration of the Libor be removed from the BBA and transferred to a new entity. The new entity turned out to be the U.S. based Intercontinental Exchange (ICE), and the BBA-Libor became temporarily known as the ICE-Libor.

The major banks responsible for the scandal—U.K's Barclays Bank, the Royal Bank of Scotland, JP Morgan Chase, the Bank of America, and Citigroup—pleaded guilty and agreed to pay approximately $6 billion in fines for their role in the scandal.

R.I.P., 2021

The ICE-Libor appeared to be a capable replacement, but the "ICE" wasn't exactly British and the "Libor" title still rankled, so in July 2017, the British Financial Conduct Authority announced that British banks would replace the Libor by the end of 2021 with a more reliable (and yet undetermined) measure. For this it appears that there will be no lack of volunteers as the Bank of England has already proposed its Sterling Overnight Index Average (Sonia), the Swiss have suggested its key swaps rate (Tois), and the United States has recommended using a Treasuries repurchase rate. So, stay tuned!

Libor	
Indicator status:	None, although it tracks the T-bill rate closely
Compiled by:	Intercontinental Exchange
Frequency:	Daily
Revisions:	None
Published data:	Most financial newspapers

Chapter 8

STOCK PRICES and
INTERNATIONAL TRADE

The Dow Jones Industrial Average

The ***Dow Jones Industrial Average (DJIA)*** is one of the oldest and most widely-quoted measures of stock market performance in the world. It is used as a proxy for the price movements of stocks issued by about 2800 companies that are primarily listed on the New York Stock Exchange (NYSE) and many that are listed on the NASDAQ.

The DJIA includes 30 representative firms, and the size of the index depends on the market price of each firm's stock at any given time. If the prices of the stocks in the average are rising, the DJIA goes up and the market is also presumed to be going up. If the prices of the 30 stocks are falling, the DJIA goes down, indicating that other stocks in the market are also presumed to be going down. Over time, some firms have been replaced to keep the list representative of changes in the economy, but the total is kept at 30.

Early History

In 1884 the Dow Jones Corporation began to publish the average closing price of 11 active stocks in its *Customer's Afternoon Letter*, a short publication that later evolved into *The Wall Street Journal*. By 1886 the average included 12 stocks, and by 1916 it was expanded to 20.[1] Finally, in 1928 it was expanded to include 30 stocks. A recent list of 30 representative stocks appears in Table 8-1.

---

[1] The Dow Jones Corporation has a complete history of the companies in the average dating from 1884 on its website at http://dowjones.com.

Table 8-1

The 30 Stocks in the Dow Jones Industrial Average

3M Company	Exxon Mobile	Microsoft
American Express	General Electric	Nike
Apple	Goldman Sachs	Pfizer
Boeing	Home Depot	Procter & Gamble
Caterpillar	IBM	Travelers Companies
Chevron	Intel	United Technologies
Cisco	Johnson & Johnson	United Health
Coca-Cola	J.P. Morgan Chase	Verizon
Disney	McDonald's	Visa
DowDuPont	Merck & Company	Wal-Mart Stores

Source: *Dow Jones Corporation*, November 10, 2017

But, Is It *Really* an Average?

In 1884 the index really was an average, but it proved difficult to maintain because of the problem caused by stock splits. For example, consider a simple DJIA which, on Monday, had three stocks priced $20, $30, and $40. The DJIA for that day would be ($20 + $30 + $40)/3 = $30, or simply 30. Next, suppose that nothing happens on Tuesday except for a two-for-one split of the $20 stock (instead of holding one share of a stock worth $20, someone now owns two shares worth $10, and so his or her wealth remains unchanged).

If we computed the simple DJIA on Tuesday by dividing the prices of three shares ($10, $30, and $40) by 3, the DJIA would drop to 26.7, even though investors would be no worse off than before. We could, however, compensate for the drop in the average by adjusting the *divisor*. Instead of dividing the sum of the prices by 3, we could divide by 2.667 so that the "average" would be ($10 + $30 + $40)/ 2.667 = $30, or 30, just as before.

Whenever a stock splits or whenever stocks on the list are replaced, the divisor can be adjusted to keep the overall average from being affected. Of course, this means that the divisor must be revised frequently and over time it can get quite small. By 1939, for example, the divisor was about 15; by 1950 it was below 9; and, by 1981 it had reached 1.3. On May 10, 2017, the divisor was 0.1460212805775, which means that the DJIA was computed as follows:

$$\text{DJIA} = \frac{\text{sum of 30 prices}}{\text{divisor}} = \frac{\$3,060.39}{0.1460212805775} = 20,958.49$$

So, we can definitely say that the Dow Jones Industrial Average really *is* an average . . . in a manner of speaking.

Are 30 Stocks Enough?

Despite the small number of stocks included in the DJIA, the companies are so large that the DJIA represents about 25 percent of the total value of all stocks on the New York Stock Exchange. As a result, movements of the DJIA coincide fairly well with those of other stock market indices that use a larger number of stocks.[2]

The 30 companies in the DJIA do not represent the smaller companies on the exchange, nor do they normally represent firms listed on any of the other regional exchanges around the country.[3] In fact, until October 1999, all of the companies in the DJIA were listed exclusively on the NYSE. The exception occurred when Intel and Microsoft, companies listed on the NASDAQ, were added in an attempt to give a bigger role to technology stocks. Later, Cisco and finally Apple, also NASDQ stocks, were added.

Why Update the DJIA?

The main reason for updating the companies in the DJIA is to make the sample more reflective of the changing conditions in the economy. For example, in April 1991, the composition of the index was changed to better reflect the size of the services sector. Navistar, Primerica, and USX were dropped from the index, while Caterpillar, Disney, and J.P. Morgan were added.

By the late 1990s, the NASDAQ was beginning to perform better than the DJIA—beating it three out of four years in a row. As a result, Intel and Microsoft took the place of Chevron and Goodyear even though they were listed on a different exchange. At the same time, Union Carbide and Sears were dropped in place of SBC Communications and Home Depot. Subsequent to that, Altria Group, Eastman Kodak, Honeywell, International Paper, and SBC Communications were dropped in favor of Bank of America, Chevron (again), Kraft Foods, Pfizer, and Verizon Communications. This

---

[2] For a long-term comparison, a chart with the DJIA and the S&P 500 in appears in Figure 8-1 on page 147.

[3] In 2008, the American Stock Exchange was absorbed by the NYSE.

means that nearly half of the 30 firms in the sample were replaced in less than 15 years, and a total of 51 firms were replaced since it was first established in 1886.

Speaking of replacement, sometimes the price of a stock can keep it out of the DJIA as was the case of Apple Computer until 2014. The price of a single Apple share in June of that year was about $650 which would have given it a disproportionate influence in the index. However a 7-for-1 split reduced the price to less than $100, and Apple was added to the DJIA a few months later even though it was listed on the NASDQ.

When firms are replaced in the DJIA, no historical revisions or other changes are made to the series. All that is done is to select a new divisor so that the DJIA remains unchanged during the transition. So, if a low-priced stock is replaced by a higher one, the divisor is increased on the following day.

Are There Other Things We Should Know?

There are two worth mentioning. First, any price-weighted average like the DJIA gives more weight to higher-priced stocks than it does to lower-priced ones. For example, a 10-percent increase in the price of 3M stock (trading near $197 in July 2017) would add $19.70 to the numerator of the above equation, while a 10-percent increase in the price of Pfizer (trading near $33 on the same day) would only add $3.30 to the numerator.

The other weakness of the DJIA is that it does not adjust for stock dividends of less than 10 percent.[4] This means that it understates long-term gains in the market. Stock prices in the DJIA will not tend to rise as fast if some companies declare relatively small but relatively frequent stock dividends.

Because the series is updated continuously and because of the visibility given to it by the Dow Jones Corporation that publishes *The Wall Street Journal*, it is a useful measure of short-term stock price movements. It is one of five major stock market indices along with

---

[4] Theoretically, a stock dividend (a dividend paid in stock rather than cash) *lowers* the company's stock price. If a firm in the 30-company sample declares an 8 percent stock dividend, the number of shares outstanding goes up by 8 percent and the price goes down by a like amount—leaving investors with no change in net wealth. However, the divisor for the DJIA remains unchanged, so the DJIA would actually show a slight decline.

the S&P 500, the Russell 3000, the Wilshire 5000 and the NASDAQ. However, when stock price movements over longer periods are of concern, researchers usually turn to other series that have a broader sample and are not biased by the issue of neglected small stock dividend payouts.

Finally, the Dow Jones Industrial Average was the first of five major stock market indices to turn down prior to the 2001 recession, although it was essentially tied with the other four when it tried to predict the arrival of the Great Recession six years and nine months later.[5]   Still, the DJIA is a reliable leading indicator for predicting future recessions, but it is not the only stock index to do so.

Dow Jones Industrial Average	
Indicator status:	Leading indicator for recessions
Compiled by:	Dow Jones & Company
Frequency:	Continuously during market hours
Revisions:	None
Published data:	*The Wall Street Journal,* the stock market section of most Newspapers; and the internet
	Economic Indicators, Council of Economic Advisors
Internet:	https://www.dowjones.com
	http://www.EconSources.com

---

[5] In 2000 all five major stock indices predicted the 2001 recession: the DJIA peaked in January; NASDAQ and the S&P 500 peaked in March; the Russell 3000 and the Wilshire 5000 both peaked in August. As for the Great Recession that began in late December 2007, the lead times were much shorter: the Wilshire 5000 turned down first in September; the S&P 500, Russell 3000, NASDAQ and DJIA all turned down in October 2007.

The Standard & Poor's 500

Perhaps the most popular measure of daily as well as long-term stock price performance is *Standard & Poor's 500* (**S&P 500**) composite index. The index represents 500 leading large-cap firms that are domiciled in the United States, are profitable according to generally accepted accounting principles (GAAP), have a $5 billion minimum market capitalization, and, have at least 50 percent of their shares reasonably priced and publicly traded on the NYSE, NASDAQ, or Bats Exchanges.

Standard and Poor's Corporation published its first market index of 233 stocks in 1923. By 1957 the list had expanded to a total of 500 firms. Today the index captures approximately 80 percent of available market capitalization of all U.S. stocks.[6]

A Family of Indices

The S&P 500 is the primary index in a family of indices, each of which is classified according to capitalization. The S&P 500 represents large-cap firms with at least $6.1 billion in capitalization. The S&P MidCap 400 represents firms with capitalizations from $1.6 billion to $6.8 billion. Finally the S&P SmallCap 600 represents firms with capitalizations from $450 million to $2.1 billion.[7] None of the companies in the MidCap 400 or SmallCap 600 overlap the S&P 500, so collectively the three "S&P U.S. indices are designed to reflect the U.S. equity markets and, through the markets, the U.S. economy".[8]

---

[6] "S&P Dow Jones Indices Fact Sheet," April 28, 2017. Market capitalization is determined by multiplying the number of tradeable public shares by their market price. So, a firm with 1 million shares trading at $15 each would have a total market capitalization of $(1,000,000)(\$15) = \$15$ million.

[7] Market capitalization guidelines are revised every 2–3 years with the most recent ones made on March 10, 2017. See "S&P U.S. Indices Methodology," *S&P Dow Jones Indices*, April 2017, for historic recapitalization dates.

[8] While the S&P 500 is our primary focus, we should note that the S&P 500 is combined with the S&P MidCap 400 and the S&P SmallCap 600 to make the S&P Composite 1500. In a similar manner, the S&P 500 is combined with the MidCap 400 to form the S&P 900, while the MidCap 400 and SmallCap 600 are combined to form the S&P 1000. See "S&P U.S. Indices Methodology," *S&P Dow Jones Indices*, April 2017.

How Is the Index Computed?

Unlike the DJIA which is a price-weighted index, the S&P 500 in Figure 8-1 is a *public float-weighted index* which reflects the total market value of all publicly traded stocks in the 500 company sample. However, the firms in the S&P 500 are not necessarily the largest ones as they are chosen to be representative of their respective industries. The industries in the index are, in descending order of weight: information technology, financials, healthcare, consumer discretionary, industrials, consumer staples, energy, utilities, real estate, materials, and telecommunication services.

The resulting valuation of the S&P 500 would be huge, of course, so the total market value of the S&P 500 is indexed to a base period of 1941−1943=10. So if the index closes at 2400, the total market value of all stocks in the S&P 500 is 240 times higher (2400/10) than it was in the base period.

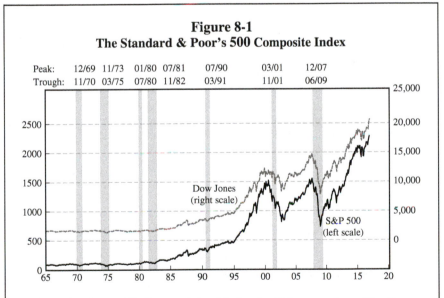

Figure 8-1
The Standard & Poor's 500 Composite Index

Peak:	12/69	11/73	01/80	07/81	07/90	03/01	12/07
Trough:	11/70	03/75	07/80	11/82	03/91	11/01	06/09

The S&P 500 is a public float-weighted index for 500 companies with a base period value of 1941−43=10, while the DJIA is a price-weighted index. Despite these differences, the two series perform fairly well as leading indicators for recessions. The S&P 500 is one of 10 components in TCB's *Leading Economic Index.*

Is the S&P 500 Better than the DJIA?

Different perhaps, but not necessarily better. If anything, it is more representative because 500 stocks are covered rather than 30. In addition, the value-weighted nature of the index means that it automatically adjusts for splits as well as for stock dividends of less than 10 percent whereas the DJIA does not.[9] However, it also appears as if the Dow Jones practice of replacing lagging stocks with more aggressive ones added some instability to the index. After all, the Dow Jones only lost 34 percent of its value because of the 2001 recession while the S&P 500 lost about 48 percent. Then, during the Great Recession, the Dow Jones lost about 54 percent of its value while the S&P 500 lost about 56 percent of its value.

Still, the S&P 500 and the DJIA both peak at about the same time, which makes them leading indicators for recessions. The S&P 500 even works so well that it is one of the 10 components used in The Conference Board's *Leading Economic Index.*[10]

Standard & Poor's 500	
Indicator status:	Leading for recessions, coincident to lagging otherwise
Compiled by:	Standard & Poor's Corporation
Frequency:	Every 15 seconds during trading days
Release date:	Daily
Revisions:	None
Published data:	Stock report listing in most daily papers
	Economic Indicators, Council of Economic Advisors
Internet:	http://www.standardandpoors.com
	http://www.EconSources.com

---

[9] Suppose that a company listed in the S&P 500 declares a 5 percent stock dividend. The number of shares would go up by 5 percent and the price of the shares would go down by a corresponding amount, leaving the total market value of the company—and the level of the S&P 500—unchanged. If that same company happened to be one of the 30 DJIA stocks, the index would fall slightly because the price of the 5 percent dividend-declaring stock in the numerator would fall, *without* any compensating change in the divisor.

[10] See The Conference Board's *Leading Economic Index* components on page 51.

The Russell 3000

Another useful measure of stock market performance is the *Russell 3000* total market index. Because it includes 3000 stocks, and because the index represents approximately 98 percent of all U.S. equity market capital, it is even more comprehensive than the S&P 500. However, and unlike most of our other economic statistics, the Russell 3000 is produced by a private, for-profit company to serve as a benchmark that can be used to evaluate the performance of other for-profit companies.[11]

Specifically, the index was designed to gauge the performance of stock fund managers who normally refer to their portfolios as "assets," or the number of shares they manage times their price. Since most portfolio managers manage hundreds or even thousands of companies with millions of shares, portfolio asset values can be huge. For this reason the Russell 3000 is a popular performance measure for stock and mutual fund managers.

How Is the Index Constructed?

First, only companies incorporated in the United States and its territories are eligible for inclusion. Next, all U.S. companies are ranked from largest to smallest according to market capitalization (number of shares outstanding times market share price). The largest 3000 companies are then used for the Russell 3000 index.[12]

The total market capitalization of 3000 stocks is huge, so the series is indexed to a December 1978 base of 100, the initial month of the series. So, if the index should close today at a value of 1580, then the total market capitalization of the largest 3000 stocks would be exactly 15.8 times higher (1580/100 = 15.8) than it was in December 1978. Day-to-day changes, or year-to-date changes, are generally reported in terms of absolute as well as percentage changes.

---

[11] The index is produced by FTSE Russell. Through a succession of mergers, the Frank Russell Company combined with the Financial Times Stock Exchange to become FTSE Russell, a private for-profit company that specializes in reports for developed, advanced merging, and emerging world equity markets.

[12] There are some exceptions: stocks trading for less than $1 a share are excluded from the survey, as are bulletin board and pink sheet stocks, limited partnerships, royalty trusts, and ADRs.

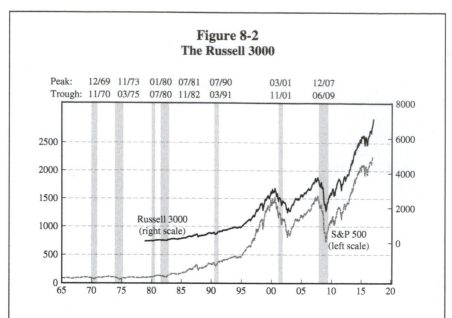

Figure 8-2
The Russell 3000

Peak: 12/69 11/73 01/80 07/81 07/90   03/01   12/07
Trough: 11/70 03/75 07/80 11/82 03/91   11/01   06/09

The Russell 3000 is a value-weighted index made up of the 3000 largest U.S. companies based on market capitalization. Like most other stock indices, it behaves as a leading indicator for recessions.

The Russell 3000 in Figure 8-2 is also divided into two other major indices. The 1000 firms with the largest capitalization make up the Russell 1000, or "large cap" index. The next 2000 firms make up the Russell 2000, or "small cap" index. The three Russell indices are like the S&P 500 in that they are market value-weighted indices. Unlike the S&P, however, no value judgments are made with respect to selecting representative firms as inclusion is based entirely on market capitalization.

How Often Is the Index Updated?

Over time, a firm's market capitalization changes whenever the price of its stock changes, or whenever the number of outstanding shares changes. In addition, there are always some mergers and bankruptcies which affect the capitalization of the 3000 companies in the series. Because of this, the index has to be reconstituted on a regular basis.

From 1979 to 1986, the indices were reconstituted quarterly and then semiannually until 1989. Since then, the indices were only adjusted annually as of May 31st market capitalizations. Russell claims that because the performance of so many mutual funds were compared to the Russell indices, that more frequent revisions would require the funds to "buy and sell stocks each time the index is reconstituted to ensure that they continue to mimic the index . . . [thereby inflicting] high transaction costs on index funds."[13]

The Historical Record

Two things are clearly evident in Figure 8-2. The first is the extent to which U.S. stock prices were hammered during the last two recessions. In 2001 the Russell 3000 lost about 44 percent of its value compared to a 48 percent loss in the S&P 500 index. During the Great Recession of 2008–09, the Russell 3000 lost 53 percent of its value whereas the S&P 500 lost about 56 percent of its value.

The second thing is that the Russell 3000, like the DJIA and the S&P 500, behaves like a leading indicator by going down just before a recession begins. The pattern is less clear for predicting subsequent recoveries, but our guess is that it will perform much like the two older and more established stock market indexes, the DJIA and the S&P 500, when it happens again.

Russell 3000	
Indicator status:	Leading for recessions
Compiled by:	FTSE Russell Company, Seattle, Washington, 98101
Frequency:	Daily
Release date:	Daily
Revisions:	Annually on May 31st
Published data:	Stock report listing in most daily papers
Internet:	http://www.ftserussell.com
	http://www.EconSources.com

---

[13] *Q&A Examining the Construction and Purpose of the Russell Indices,* www.russell.com, July 12, 2003.

The Wilshire 5000

Another broad measure of overall stock market performance is provided by the **Wilshire 5000**. The index was designed as a comprehensive market measure that covers all U.S. stocks, making it "the first and oldest measure of the total U.S equity market." In fact, Wilshire prides itself on being "the most pure and complete measure of the entire U.S. stock market.[14]

The Wilshire 5000 was created in 1974 with time series going back to 1971.[15] Like the Russell 3000, the Wilshire 5000 is produced by a for-profit company, and in addition to being a comprehensive measure of U.S. equity markets, the index is often used as a benchmark to compare the performance of stock and mutual fund managers to the broader market.

How Is the Index Constructed?

When first created, there were approximately 5000 companies in the index, hence the name. But, recessions, IPOs, mergers, and bankruptcies have caused the actual number of companies to fluctuate from a low of 3069 to a high of 7562 to about 3500 in the second quarter of 2017.[16]

There are two major versions of the Wilshire 5000. One is a price index, shown in Figure 8-3, which approximates dollar value changes of U.S. equity markets, and a "total" index that is a float-adjusted full market cap. Both behave about the same, but for comparison purposes with the S&P 500, we prefer the price index.

Are All U.S. Stocks in the Index?

Not all. To be included in the index, a company must have its primary market listing issue in the United States. In addition to

---

[14] "Wilshire 5000 Total Market Index Fact Sheet" March 31, 2017.

[15] For a brief history of the Wilshire 5000, see information provided by Wikipedia at: https://en.wikipedia.org/wiki/Wilshire_5000.

[16] "Wilshire 5000: Myths and Misconceptions," and "Wilshire Fundamental Characteristics," March 31, 2017.

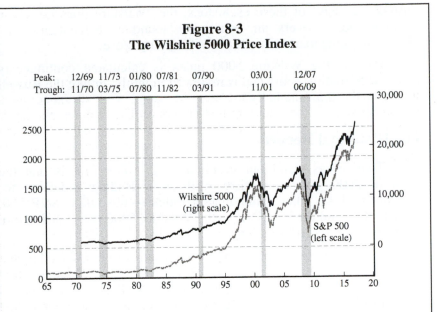

Figure 8-3
The Wilshire 5000 Price Index

The Wilshire 5000 price index is used to measure the dollar changes of all U.S. equity markets. The number of firms varies with changes in economic conditions, but the number of firms in the index are reviewed monthly and the index is calculated continuously during U.S. trading market hours.

common stocks, a firm can also be included if it is a real estate investment trust (REIT) or limited partnership. If a company has more than one class of stock, the various stock issues are combined into a primary issue for purposes of computing the total float-adjusted market capitalization (the number of publicly available shares times their market value).[17] Finally, only U.S. equities with "readily available prices" are listed. To determine this, Wilshire requires that a stock must be traded daily to have readily available prices.

In addition to excluding stocks that do not have readily available prices, additional categories of excluded equities include pink sheets,[18] closely held public stock, and other issues for technical

[17] "Wilshire 5000 Total Market Index Fact Sheet" March 31, 2017.

[18] Pink sheet stocks are typically low value stocks that do not meet the requirements to be listed on a major exchange, do not file reports with the SEC, and seldom make their balance sheets and financial information public.

reasons. Because of these exclusions, the "Wilshire does not claim that the index covers an impressive sounding percentage (e.g., 98 percent of the market,"[19] although it is pretty close.

Finally, the Wilshire 5000 index is calculated continuously during U.S. trading hours and is reviewed monthly, unlike the Russell 3000 which is done annually.

The Historical Record

Two things stand out in Figure 8-3. The first is that the Wilshire 5000 performs fairly well as a leading indicator for recessions. Like other major market indices—the DJIA, S&P 500, Russell 3000 and the NASDAQ—the Wilshire 5000 peaks just before the economy enters a recession.[20]

The second is the way in which both series were affected by the last two recessions. Because of the 2001 recession, the Wilshire 5000 lost about 46 percent of its value while the S&P 500 lost about 48 percent of its. And, because of the Great Recession, the Wilshire lost about 52 percent of its value while the S&P 500 lost about 56 percent of its value. It's hard to draw a conclusion here, but if anything it almost appears as if there's not much difference between the performance of the two series.

The Wilshire 5000	
Indicator status:	Leading indicator for recessions
Compiled by:	Wilshire Associates, Inc., New York, NY 10022
Frequency:	Daily
Release date:	Daily
Revisions:	None
Published data:	Stock report listing in most daily papers or on the web
Internet:	http://www.wilshire.com/indexes

---

[19] "Wilshire 5000: Myths and Misconceptions," November 2014.
[20] See footnote 5 for more details on the lengths of lead times for the DJIA, the S&P 500, the Russell 3000, the Wilshire 5000, and the NASDAQ.

The NASDAQ Composite

On February 8, 1971, NASDAQ, the National Association of Security Dealers Automated Quotation, became the first electronic stock exchange. Today the **NASDAQ Composite** is the primary index reporting on about 3000 NASDAQ listed securities.

At the time of NASDAQ's founding, the New York Stock Exchange, the American Exchange, and every other organized stock exchange required traders to meet on the exchange "floor" as a requirement for executing a trade. However, not all stocks are traded on organized exchanges. As late as 2014 it was estimated that as many as 40 percent of U.S. stock trades took place in "off-exchange trading" locations.[21] Many of these stocks were deemed to be speculative in nature, had low prices, or had other characteristics that would prevent them from being registered on a major stock exchange.

Because the NASDAQ was successful in establishing an efficient computerized trading market that suited the needs of many over-the-counter (OTC) companies, trade volume increased dramatically and the NASDAQ soon became the second largest exchange in the world behind only the New York Stock Exchange.[22] Companies such as Apple, Microsoft, Cisco, Oracle and Dell helped fuel NASDAQ's popularity during this period of rapid growth.

NASDAQ Eligibility Requirements

To join NASDAQ, a company must be exclusively listed on the NASDAQ stock market exchange, although exceptions were made for companies listed on other exchanges prior to January 1, 2004. In addition, companies in the NASDAQ can be domestic or international as there are no restrictions with regard to domicile.

The specific types of securities eligible for the NASDAQ "include common stocks ordinary shares, ADRs, shares of beneficial interest or limited partnership interests, and tracking stocks. Securities

---

[21] McCrank, John, "Dark markets may be more harmful than high-frequency trading," Reuters, 12 April 2014.
[22] "Monthly Reports," World-Exchanges.org. World Federation of Exchanges, 17 August 2014.

not included in the index are closed end funds, convertible debentures, exchange traded funds, preferred stocks, rights, warrants, units and other derivative securities."[23]

The Historical Record

Figure 8-4 shows the NASDAQ composite index series from its origins in 1971 until 2017. The index uses a market capital weighting methodology which makes the composite's value equal to the sum of all shares outstanding times each security's price. The series is then indexed to a February 5, 1971 base of 100 to make the numbers manageable.

Like most other major stock indices, the NASDAQ peaks just before a recession begins which makes it a leading indicator for predicting downturns.[24] It also reaches a trough shortly after or during a recession

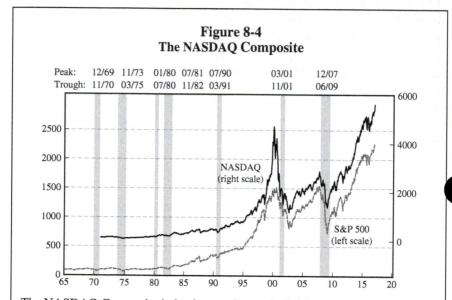

Figure 8-4
The NASDAQ Composite

| Peak: | 12/69 | 11/73 | 01/80 | 07/81 | 07/90 | 03/01 | 12/07 |
| Trough: | 11/70 | 03/75 | 07/80 | 11/82 | 03/91 | 11/01 | 06/09 |

The NASDAQ Composite index is a market capitalization-weighted index of approximately 3000 common equities, American deposit receipts (ADRs), real estate investment trusts (REITs), and limited partnership interests that are listed on the NASDAQ exchange.

---

[23] "NASDAQ, Composite Index Methodology," NASDAQ INC, January 2012.
[24] See footnote 5 for more specifics on the lead times of the major stock market indicators.

which doesn't give it any particular leading or lagging indicator characteristics for the ensuing recovery.

Perhaps the most striking thing evident in Figure 8-4 is the dramatic appearance of the dot-com bubble that occurred from about 1997 to 2001. This was a period of historically rapid growth and speculation in the technology industry that famously collapsed just prior to the 2001 recession. Because so many new technology stocks were listed on the NASDAQ, it increased much faster and then collapsed much further then did the older and more steadfast S&P 500. During its precipitous decline, the NASDAQ lost about 75 percent of its value while the S&P 500 lost about 48 percent of its value.

By the time of the Great Recession of 2008–09, the differences between the losses of all major stock indices were much closer: with the S&P 500 having lost about 56 percent of its value; NASDAQ having lost 55 percent of its; the Dow Jones having lost 54 percent; the Russell 3000 having lost 53 percent; and, the Wilshire 5000 having lost about 52 percent of its index values.

Clearly the NASDAQ had matured after its seemingly wild-west days during the dot-com period. Either that or speculators had become much more adept at exploiting arbitrage differences between the various exchanges.

The NASDAQ Composite

Indicator status:	Leading indicator for recessions
Compiled by:	NASDAQ Inc., One Liberty Plaza, 165 Broadway, NY, New York 10006
Frequency:	Daily
Release date:	Daily
Revisions:	None
Published data:	Stock report listing in most daily papers or on the web
Internet:	http://www.NASDAQ.com

The Balance of Trade

When a country engages in international trade, several formal sets of accounts are used to track the flow of international transactions. The *balance on goods and services* that replaced the *balance on merchandise trade* account in 1994 is perhaps the best known series.[25] The word "balance" in the title allows for the possibility of a surplus as well as a deficit. However, because U.S. imports have exceeded U.S. exports for so long, our international trade statistics are commonly—although improperly—called the *deficit on goods and services* accounts.

NIPA (Again)

Trade statistics, like many other statistics generated by the U.S. Department of Commerce, are directly related to the national income and product accounts (NIPA). Table 8-2, a version of Table 2-4 on page 28, follows the familiar approach of dividing the economy into sectors. This time we want to focus on the foreign sector, otherwise known as "Net exports of goods and services," to see how the *balance on goods and services* is computed.

In Table 8-2, the advanced first-quarter estimate in current dollars for all exports was $2316.2 billion. This was offset by imports of $2874.6 billion, leaving a $558.4 billion deficit in the balance on goods and services. These numbers are reported on an annualized basis and show the net balance that would occur if exports and imports remained unchanged at the current rate for the entire year. The export and import categories are further divided into goods (merchandise) and services, with the table showing goods exports of $1519.6 billion and imports of $2354.4 billion—from which we can calculate (but do not show) a $834.8 billion deficit on goods alone. This $834.8 billion is the *balance on merchandise trade* which has been in continuous deficit since the first quarter of 1976. Annualized figures such as those shown in Table 8-2 are estimated by the BEA and published as part of the NIPA even though the year is not yet over.

---

[25] At the time, the services component of the trade balance was running a substantial surplus so the overall impact of combining goods with services was to sharply reduce the trade deficit.

Table 8-2
NIPA and the Goods and Services Trade Balance, Billions of Dollars

	Current	Chained (2009$)	% GDP
Gross domestic product	*$19,007.3*	*$16,842.4*	*100.0*
Personal consumption expenditures	*13,096.4*	*11,679.5*	*68.9*
Gross private domestic investment	*3,146.5*	*2,898.4*	*16.6*
Net exports of goods and services	*(558.4)*	*(602.7)*	*(2.9)*
Exports	2,316.2	2,167.5	12.2
Goods	1,519.6	1,482.8	8.0
Services	796.6	685.8	4.2
Imports	2,874.6	2,770.3	15.1
Goods	2,354.4	2,279.7	12.4
Services	520.1	488.3	2.7
Government consumption & gross investment	*3,322.7*	*2,895.2*	*17.5*

Source: *Bureau of Economic Analysis.* First quarter 2017 advance estimates; some totals may not add due to rounding.

Collecting and Reporting the Data

In practice, data for exports and imports of goods are collected continuously by the Census Bureau from declarations filed with the U.S. Customs Office by international shippers. Other techniques are used to estimate the monthly volume of services. Because of the nature of the data, trade figures are normally released 45 days after the close of the reference month.

The Census Bureau releases trade figures in several formats. Initial trade figures are reported monthly, and year-to-date figures are obtained by adding up the trade balances for the required number of months. And, because of the way the data are summed in the trade deficit reports, the numbers will be small if for the month, approximately three times larger if the report is for the quarter, and approximately 12 times larger if the numbers are annual. Accordingly, we have to be careful not to confuse a relatively large monthly figure with a relatively small quarterly one—or even annualized ones like those in Table 8-2.

Are the Annualized NIPA Data Enough?

Not always. The problem is that we still don't have the whole international picture unless we look at the *balance on current account* which requires three further adjustments to the net exports of goods and services. First, we have to add income generated from U.S. assets held abroad. Second, we must subtract any payments made because of foreign assets in the United States. Third, we have to take into account net unilateral transfers made abroad: government grants to other nations; pension and social security payments to people living in other countries; and, payments made by private individuals to family members, political organizations, and religious movements in other countries.[26]

Because of the difficulties posed by these adjustments, annualized data like those in Table 8-2 are usually sufficient for most purposes, even though they don't present a complete picture of our trade balance.

When plotted from 1958 to the present, as in Figure 8-5, we get a mostly complete picture of our long-term trade deficit. The balance can either be shown as the difference between overall goods and services exports and imports (shown at the top of the graph), or it can be plotted separately as shown in the bottom of the figure.

Despite the more comprehensive measure provided by the current account balance, the balance on goods and services shown in Figure 8-5 is perhaps our primary international trade statistic, or at least the one that gets the most attention. The trade figures on goods and services are important because they affect the value of the U.S. dollar and therefore employment in the export and import industries.

Should We Try to Fix a Trade Deficit?

Probably not. This is because the deficit usually tends to be self-correcting. For example, a weak dollar causes exports to rise faster than imports, which causes the trade balance to improve. Eventually, fewer dollars going abroad relative to other currencies causes the value of the dollar to rise, which reverses the trend in exports and imports and worsens the trade balance. Consequently, any legislative effort to correct a trade deficit will hurt importers and consumers who benefit from low import prices, although it will

---

[26] It also takes more time to get an accurate balance on current account report because of the time it takes to get these additional numbers.

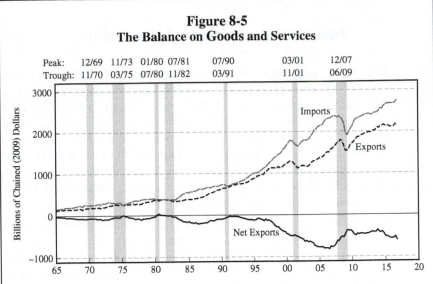

Figure 8-5
The Balance on Goods and Services

| Peak: | 12/69 | 11/73 | 01/80 | 07/81 | 07/90 | 03/01 | 12/07 |
| Trough: | 11/70 | 03/75 | 07/80 | 11/82 | 03/91 | 11/01 | 06/09 |

The balance on goods and services can be shown as the difference between exports and imports in the top part of figure, or plotted separately as in the lower part of the figure. Either way, the balance on goods and services has been negative ever since the early 1990s.

benefit exporters. Any effort to correct a trade surplus will have the opposite effects. So rather than pick their poison, politicians usually choose to let the market take care of any trade imbalances.

Balance on Goods and Services	
Indicator status:	None
Compiled by:	Census Bureau
Frequency:	Monthly, quarterly
Release date:	45 days after close of reporting month
Revisions:	One month back for seasonally adjusted data; 6 months back for constant dollar series
Published data:	Report FT900, Census Bureau
	Economic Indicators, Council of Economic Advisors
Internet:	https://www.census.gov/foreign-trade/index.html
	http://www.EconSources.com

International Value of the Dollar

When we talk about the value of the U.S. dollar, we are referring to its purchasing power relative to other currencies. However, we can't evaluate the dollar's strength by comparing it to just one or two exchange rates. Instead, we have to see how the dollar performs against a broad range of currencies. This first became a problem in 1971 when President Richard Nixon abruptly and unilaterally announced that the United States would no longer redeem foreign-held U.S. dollars for gold, thus ending the remnants of a U.S. gold standard and a long era of fixed exchange rates.

The first attempt to compile an international currency index using a group of major industrialized countries was done by the Fed and called the called the G-10, illustrated in Figure 8-6.[27] The G-10 weight of each country's currency was based on the amount of global trade each one had relative to the other countries in 1971, the year flexible exchange rates were adopted.

Out With the Old . . .

When first introduced, the G-10 served as the main measure of the dollar's strength. The series went up when the dollar got stronger, and went down when the dollar got weaker relative to the other 10 currencies.

Since 1971, however, world trade patterns have changed and currency evolutions such as the emergence of the European Union's euro have taken place. As a result, the Fed retired its initial G-10 currency series and replaced it with three new trade-weighted ones: the *broad currency index*, the *major currency index*, and the *other important trading partners* (*OITP*) index. All three series, indexed to a base of 100, appear in Figures 8-6 and 8-7.

---

[27] The ten countries were Belgium, Canada, France, Germany, Italy, Japan, Netherlands, Sweden, Switzerland and the United Kingdom. The measure was first called the *exchange*, or *trade-weighted value of the U.S. dollar*. The Fed's use of the term "G-10" did not seem to come into use until after the Fed introduced its new broad currency measures.

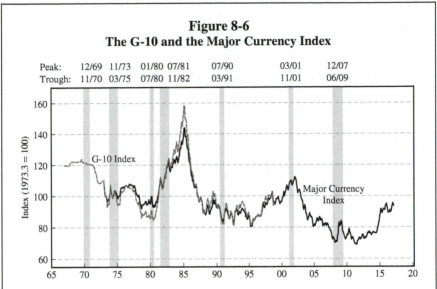

Figure 8-6
The G-10 and the Major Currency Index

Peak:	12/69	11/73	01/80 07/81	07/90	03/01	12/07
Trough:	11/70	03/75	07/80 11/82	03/91	11/01	06/09

The *G-10 index*, formerly known as the *exchange value of the U.S. dollar*, was our most comprehensive measure of the dollar's international strength until it was discontinued in 1998 and replaced by the *major currency index*.

... And In With the New

The G-10 replacement, the ***major currency index***, is a weighted average of seven currencies from the following: the Euro area, Australia, Canada, Japan, Sweden, Switzerland, and the United Kingdom. The major currency index covers 22 countries and is shown in Figure 8-6 along with the G-10. Even though the weighting and sample sizes are different, it is clear that the relative strength of the U.S. dollar is about the same in both currency measures.

The second major index, the ***broad currency index,*** is made up of approximately 26 currencies. Unlike the G-10, weights are not fixed, but are adjusted over time as trade patterns change.[28]

---

[28] The broad currency index is a weighted average of the U.S. dollar against the following currencies: the Euro area, Argentina, Australia, Brazil, Canada, Chile, China, Colombia, Hong Kong, India, Indonesia, Israel, Japan, Korea, Malaysia, Mexico, Philippines, Russia, Saudi Arabia, Singapore, Sweden, Switzerland, Taiwan, Thailand, United Kingdom, and Venezuela.

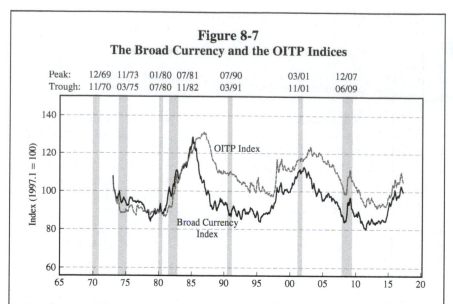

Figure 8-7
The Broad Currency and the OITP Indices

The *broad currency index* is now the most comprehensive measure of the international value of the dollar. The series includes both the *major currency index* and the *other important trading partners* (OITP) index.

When the broad currency index was initially introduced, it had a value of 32 in 1973 and then increased steadily after that. While this may seem odd, the broad index contained a number of high-inflation countries that experienced severe currency depreciations that drove up the demand for the dollar. However, when the broad currency index is converted to real or inflation-adjusted values, as in Figure 8-7, a more stable purchasing power of the U.S. dollar is apparent, with the dollar being relatively strong in the mid-1980s, the early 2000s, and again after 2015.[29]

The last series is the **OITP currency index**, which is short for "other important trading partners." This index, also shown in Figure 8-7, consists of 19 countries that are in the broad index, but not in the major currency index. Many of these countries' currencies are not traded extensively outside their home markets, although they are still important U.S. trading partners. The OITP index is also computed in real or price-adjusted terms and indexed to a base value of January 1997=100.

---

[29] Converting to an index changed the initial 1973 index value of 32 to 100.

So Why Are These Series Important?

Because, the large changes in the international value of the dollar shown in Figures 8-6 and 8-7 have an enormous impact on the prices we pay and on employment in the nation's export and import industries.

When the purchasing power of the dollar is high, as in the mid-1980s, foreign goods and services are relatively inexpensive resulting in a large number of imports, happy consumers, and expanded employment in those industries that are involved with imports. At the same time, however, American products are much more expensive abroad, leading to declines in exports and layoffs in the export industries. These forces are reversed when the value of the dollar falls, as it did in the early 1990s and again in 2012–15. Consequently, the result of a widely fluctuating dollar is a feast or famine situation for everyone in the import or export industries as the dollar goes from strength to weakness, and then eventually back to strength again.

These forces also affect the overall balance of trade. When the value of the dollar is high, more imports and fewer exports worsen the balance of trade. When the value of the dollar is low, the situation reverses itself, resulting in an improvement in the trade balance.

International Value of the U.S. Dollar

Indicator status:	None
Compiled by:	Federal Reserve Board of Governors
Frequency:	*H.10* weekly; *G.5* monthly
Release date:	*H.10* Monday for the previous week ending Friday; *G.5* last day of month for the reporting month
Revisions:	None
Published data:	*Federal Reserve Bulletin,* Fed Board of Governors
	Statistical Release G.5, for monthly rates
	Statistical Release H.10, for daily rates
Internet:	http://www.federalreserve.gov
	http://www.EconSources.com

Foreign Exchange

Foreign exchange, in the context of international trade or finance, usually refers to the number of foreign currency units that can be purchased with one U.S. dollar. For example, we might say that the U.S. dollar is worth 112.84 Japanese yen. The amount of a specific foreign currency that can be purchased with the dollar is called the ***foreign exchange rate***, and there are well over 200 exchange rates for the U.S. dollar in the world today.

Currency Units per Dollar and Dollar Equivalents

One popular way to express an exchange rate is in *American terms*, or in the number of U.S. dollars needed to buy a single foreign currency unit. In Table 8-3 for example, if one euro costs $1.09278, then 1.09278 is the U.S. dollar equivalent of one euro. Likewise, if the cost of a single yen is $0.00886, the U.S. dollar equivalent of one yen is 0.00886.

Table 8-3
Selected Foreign Exchange Rates

	U.S. $ Equivalents (American terms)	Foreign Currency Units per U.S. $ (European terms)
Japan (Yen)	0.00886	112.8400
Mexico (peso)	0.05234	19.1055
Switzerland (SFranc)	1.00210	0.9979
U.K. (Pound)	1.29416	0.7727
E.U. (Euro)	1.09278	0.9151

Source: *Foreign Exchange Rates – H.10,* data are for May 8, 2017.

The second way to express an exchange rate is in *European terms*, or in the number of foreign currency units that are equal to one U.S. dollar. The two terms are simply reciprocals and are shown in Table 8-3 above.[30] For example, if one British pound costs $1.29416, then $1 is worth 0.7727 pounds (0.7727 is the reciprocal of 1.29416).

---

[30] Some reciprocals may not match because of rounding.

Likewise, if one yen costs $0.00886 in American terms, then the value of $1 is 112.8400 yen (the reciprocal of .00886).

Currency Cross Rates

If we want to know the exchange rate between two currencies, we could express everything in terms of cross rates, as in Table 8-4. This is especially helpful when neither of the currencies being traded is the U.S. dollar.

Table 8-4
Currency Cross Rates

	U.S. $	Euro	Pound	SFranc	Peso	Yen
Japan	112.8400	123.30893	146.03339	113.07746	5.90615	—.—
Mexico	19.1055	20.87805	24.72564	19.14571	—.—	0.16932
Switzerland	0.9979	1.09048	1.29145	—.—	0.05223	0.00884
U.K.	0.7727	0.84439	—.—	0.77433	0.04044	0.00685
Euro	0.9151	—.—	1.18425	0.91703	0.04790	0.00811
U.S.	—.—	1.09278	1.29416	1.00210	0.05234	0.00886

Source: Computed from Table 8-3 (reciprocals may not match due to rounding)

In the table, the value of each currency unit is expressed in terms of other currencies. For example, if one U.S. dollar buys 0.9979 Swiss Francs, and if one U.S. dollar buys 19.1055 Mexican pesos, then one SFranc is worth 19.1055/0.9979 = 19.14571 Mexican pesos. Likewise, if a dollar can purchase 112.8400 yen, and if a dollar can purchase 0.9151 euros, then one euro is worth 123.30893 Japanese yen (112.8400/.9151 = 123.30893).

Foreign Exchange Rates

Indicator status:	None
Compiled by:	Federal Reserve Board of Governors
Frequency:	*Statistical Releases G.5* monthly; *H.10* weekly
Release date:	*H.10* Monday for the previous week ending Friday; *G.5* last day of month for the reporting month
Revisions:	None
Published data:	*The Wall Street Journal* for previous the day *Statistical Release H.10*, for daily NYC noon buying rates
Internet:	http://www.federalreserve.gov http://www.EconSources.com

Appendix

Chain Weighting

Chain-weighted calculations are hardly intuitive, so they are probably best explained with an example such as the one in Table 1 below which has only two product groups: computers and everything else. Before we begin, we should note that the examples are loosely modeled after Table 2-1 on page 14 of the text. You may want to review that table first before proceeding.

In the first year of our abbreviated economy in Table 1, 2 units (Q) of computers are sold at an average price (P) of $10. Five units of everything else are sold at $10, generating a first-year GDP of $70. Similar calculations for the next year show a new GDP of $99, a 41.43 percent gain over the first. In tabular form, the data would look like this:

Table 1
GDP Growth in Current Dollars

Year 1				Year 2			
	Q	P	(P)(Q)		Q	P	(P)(Q)
Computers:	2	$10	$20	Computers:	4	$6	$24
Everything Else:	5	10	50	Everything Else:	5	15	75
			GDP = $70				GDP = $99

One-year growth in GDP = $99/$70 = 1.4143, or 41.43%

And yet, a closer look at Year 2 reveals that the robust 41.43 percent growth was due almost entirely to inflation in the "everything else" category. In fact, because computer prices went down so much, consumers only spent $4 more on computers in year 2 than they did in the previous year.

If we try to compensate for inflation by using fixed base-year prices from the first year, as in Table 2, we can see that the estimated growth for GDP is quite different, and much lower:

Table 2
GDP Growth Using Constant (Year 1) Prices

Year 1				Year 2			
	Q	P	(P)(Q)		Q	P	(P)(Q)
Computers:	2	$10	$20	Computers:	4	$10	$40
Everything Else:	5	10	50	Everything Else:	5	10	50
		GDP =	$70			GDP =	$90

One-year growth in GDP = $90/$70 = 1.2857, or 28.57%

Or, we could compute GDP growth using constant year 2 prices as in Table 3, which gives us an even *lower* growth estimate:

Table 3
GDP Growth Using Constant (Year 2) Prices

Year 1				Year 2			
	Q	P	(P)(Q)		Q	P	(P)(Q)
Computers:	2	$6	$12	Computers:	4	$6	$24
Everything Else:	5	15	75	Everything Else:	5	15	75
		GDP =	$87			GDP =	$99

One-year growth in GDP = $99/$87 = 1.1379, or 13.79%

If we want to adjust for inflation by using a set of fixed or base year prices, which of the two methods is theoretically superior: estimates using first year prices, or estimates using second year prices? Both have advantages and disadvantages, but it is clear that there is a "weighting effect"—a distortion that takes place because those quantities which have increased the most are usually associated with goods, such as computers, whose prices have declined the most relative to other prices.

The solution to the problem of the optimal base year is to find the geometric mean of the two index numbers. This is done by computing the square root of their product. In other words, the computations would appear as:

$$\sqrt{(1.2857)(1.1379)} = 1.2095, \text{ or } 20.95\%$$

This geometric average is also called the "Fisher Ideal" index number, and is the basis for BEA's chain-weighted prices that are now used in place of the fixed base-year weighted prices employed until 1995.[1]

Despite the theoretical superiority of the geometric mean, BEA's changeover at the beginning of 1996 was not without controversy. For example, second quarter growth in 1995, formerly reported at +0.5 percent, was revised downward by 0.7 percent to −0.2 percent. Likewise, the revisions also meant that the growth of real GDP during the 2001–2005 expansion was actually 0.5 percent less than previously reported.

---

[1] For a nice example of a simple geometric mean, see the short example by W. L. Silber at New York University: http://people.stern.nyu.edu/wsilber/Geometric Average Versus Arithmetic Average.pdf

Index